The Stage Directions Guide to Shakespeare

Edited by

Stephen Peithman
Neil Offen

HEINEMANN
Portsmouth, NH

HEINEMANN
A division of Reed Elsevier Inc.
361 Hanover Street
Portsmouth, NH 03801–3912
www.heinemanndrama.com

Offices and agents throughout the world

LIBRARY OF CONGRESS CATALOGING-IN-PUBLICATION DATA
The Stage directions guide to Shakespeare / edited by Stephen Peithman, Neil Offen.
    p. cm.
    Based chiefly on articles originally appearing in the periodical Stage directions.
    ISBN 0-325-00233-9
    1. Shakespeare, William, 1564–1616—Dramatic production.
  2. Shakespeare, William, 1564–1616—Stage history.
  3. Theater—Production and direction.   4. Stage directions.
  I. Title: Guide to Shakespeare.   II. Peithman, Stephen.
  III. Offen, Neil.   IV. Stage directions.
  PR3091.S687   2000
  792.9'5—dc21

                                    00-038878

Editor: Lisa A. Barnett
Production: Abigail M. Heim
Cover design: Barbara Werden
Cover photo: Rob Karosis
Manufacturing: Louise Richardson

Printed in the United States of America on acid-free paper

04   03   02   01   00   DA   1   2   3   4   5

The Stage Directions
Guide to
Shakespeare

Heinemann's STAGE DIRECTIONS Series

For all those in front of the lights and behind the scenes
who understand the magic of theater

Contents

Foreword

*H*e died nearly four hundred years ago, and his death was barely noticed. We don't know if he died a natural death or was murdered, as some still claim. We are not exactly sure where he was born and not even positive about the date of his birth. We are not certain where he attended school or even *if* he attended school. We don't know how he spent a good portion of his life, and despite the fact that his name has become an adjective, we can't be entirely confident that we even know how he spelled that last name. Perhaps most confoundingly, we can't really be absolutely positive that he wrote everything we think he wrote. Maybe the words were Christopher Marlowe's or Francis Bacon's or the Earl of Oxford's, after all.

Yet, somehow, it doesn't matter. What does matter is the work, and because of the work, William Shakespeare is as alive today to us as he was to his Elizabethan contemporaries four hundred years ago. He lives, of course, through his plays that we mount and go to see again and again. He lives through the raucous humor of *A Midsummer Night's Dream* and through the wrenching emotions of *King Lear*. He speaks to us still today through the existential quandaries of

Hamlet and the still contemporary intrigues of *The Taming of the Shrew*.

In the theater, Shakespeare is the ultimate to which we aspire. Although his plays during his time were simply popular entertainment, today they are a measuring stick. Whether we do *only* the Bard's work, a whole season of his plays, or just the occasional Shakespearean performance, he is the measure against which we compare ourselves. His works demand that we be at our very best.

His works confront us with questions. Are our actors good enough to handle Shakespeare? Can they do the right accents, can they move the right way? Can our designers create appropriate sets and costumes? Can our director say something new or different about a work that has been produced for centuries and that everyone knows? Can the director stage the fights and battles that are so intrinsic to Shakespeare? Will our audiences understand the language? Will they be interested in a work that—on the surface—may appear to be dated and not speak to them directly? Can we find a way to make them interested, to bring them to the theater? Can we show them that Shakespeare is as funny as Neil Simon, as intriguing as Tom Stoppard, as contemporary as Tony Kushner?

To answer all these questions, the editors of *Stage Directions* magazine have gathered together in this book a wide variety of material on the subject of the Bard that has appeared in the magazine since its founding in 1988. We have assembled interviews with perceptive and experienced Shakespearean directors, producers, actors, and designers, along with articles by those who have been involved in Shakespearean productions themselves. We have blended all this with our own knowledge and experience and our readings of material from companies throughout the country.

After a look at the most obvious question involved in mounting a Shakespearean production—Why should you mount one?—the book then takes a look at the most significant directorial decisions involved in such a production, including how to decide about where and when to set the play and whether you need to cut the text. We then look at Shakespeare from the actor's perspective, examining not just how to perform the Bard, but also how to move like an Elizabethan and even fight like one. Once your play is ready, then you may need advice on how to publicize your Shakespearean production, how to teach—and learn—Shakespeare, and how to do the Bard on a budget, among other topics. For those companies that may venture into Shakespearean production only once a year or even less often, some useful lessons can be learned from institutions that focus exclusively, or nearly so, on the Bard. Finally, our "Did You Know?" section offers a wide variety of tidbits on Shakespearean production, from making sure of your shoes to watching your hair.

Whether you have never—yet—put on a play by William Shakespeare or have already mounted every work from *Titus Andronicus* to *Pericles*, we hope that this book will offer you a new practical perspective on the greatest and most popular playwright of all time.

About Stage Directions *and This Book*

The majority of the material in this book is based on information that first appeared in the pages of *Stage Directions*, the "practical magazine of theater." Since 1988, *Stage Directions* has published articles on a wide range of subject matter—not only mounting Shakespearean productions, but also acting and directing in general, as well as management, publicity, scenic and costume design, lighting and special effects, and much more.

During that time, we've taken a close look at almost every aspect of putting on a Shakespearean play. We've put all that advice together in this book, updated and revised as needed, and added introductions that help put the information into perspective.

As we do with our magazine, we'd like to hear your comments on this book or suggestions for future topics in our expanding library of *Stage Directions* books that already include *The Stage Directions Guide to Directing, The Stage Directions Guide to Getting and Keeping Your Audience, The Stage Directions Guide to Auditions,* and *The Stage Directions Guide to Publicity*. Please write to us c/o Heinemann, 361 Hanover Street, Portsmouth, NH 03801-3912.

Stephen Peithman
Neil Offen

The Stage Directions
Guide to
Shakespeare

Introduction

L et's face what is an almost inarguable truth: many companies produce works by William Shakespeare mainly because they are free. (It's the same reason, of course, that so much Gilbert & Sullivan is produced.) Having been written four hundred years ago, Shakespeare's plays are no longer under copyright and no royalties must be paid for their use. And not being under copyright, they are also malleable: you can cut them and change them and re-arrange them as you will, and not have to answer to any difficult author and his publishing company and their lawyers. You can meld it to your particular stage, your scenic requirements, your actors' capabilities. Whether you are a just-starting-out community theater group, a university-based theatrical organization, or a well-to-do, well-respected regional theater, a flexible play without royalties is a boon to any season.

There are also companies, to be sure, that choose to mount a Shakespearean production because they think they must. A *Macbeth* or a *Henry IV*, they believe, will give them an aura of seriousness, of classicism. It will look good, so to speak, on their resumé. It will impress their audiences and—perhaps more importantly—their boards of directors and financial angels.

Yet no company, producer, director, actor, or designer should feel obligated to do Shakespeare. It is not a penance you must pay to be taken seriously. By the same token, no one should be dissuaded from tackling Shakespeare by the belief that the work is too serious, too classic, too difficult to do and do well.

While the absence of royalties and the flexibility of the scripts can be important reasons, they pale in significance before the most important rationale for doing the works of Shakespeare: they are wonderful, enthralling plays, the epitome of theatrical art. Depending on the particular work, they are funny, insightful, touching, emotionally demanding, perceptive, clever, lyrical, and much, much more. They are, in fact, the height of theatrical art—and if theater is what you do, then Shakespeare is the height of your aspirations.

Yet not all audiences share that opinion. Just because some of us may be passionate about Shakespeare doesn't mean that everyone else is. While the Bard may be the most popular playwright the world has ever known, sometimes we may have to convince theatergoers and members of our companies of that fact. We all need to remember that Shakespeare was a popular playwright; he wrote for the masses, to entertain the boisterous audiences of the Rose and the Globe theaters. His plays had to offer popular entertainment; they were the Hollywood movies of their day.

However, one shouldn't assume, therefore, that they are easy productions to mount. After all, they are plays written a long time ago, under different circumstances, in what is almost a different language, in verse, with different reference points, and under different constraints (for example, they were designed to be performed in theaters that were completely in-the-round). They require multiple skills from the directors and the actors and all those involved in the production—even if you're setting the play in a hairdresser's salon in 1950s Alabama.

It really doesn't matter where or when one of the Bard's plays is set. What does matter, above all, is that the production show us the understanding and intelligence, the wit and the perception that have distinguished the works of Shakespeare since they were first put on in London.

THE QUESTION IS WHY

Why should your company put on a Shakespearean play?

Although the Bard has endured for four hundred years, he's not on television every night or always on Broadway or in the gossip columns, and he might, after all, be a tough sell to your audience. The language could be a problem and the casting process could be onerous. The plays can be difficult, requiring more skill and commitment from everyone than, perhaps, a less-demanding modern play might. Who said you had to do Shakespeare's plays, anyway?

The first answer to all those questions might be, of course, that the works of Shakespeare are in the public domain, which means that no royalties have to be paid for producing any of his plays. Undoubtedly, many companies initially decide to mount a Shakespearean production for this reason: the Bard is cheap. Add to that the fact that Shakespeare can be played in street clothes and without significant sets (as was the case, in fact, in Elizabethan times), and a production of one of the plays can be very economical indeed. When you've just had to lay out some serious cash for the rights to a Neil Simon or a

Rodgers & Hammerstein, Shakespeare can suddenly seem very attractive—particularly to the board of directors.

But mounting a production of any play—and surely, one by Shakespeare—exclusively for financial concerns would be a serious mistake. The commitment necessary to put on, say, *Richard III*, demands more than just a pecuniary motive. So, then, considering all the difficulties, all the demands, why do it?

Well-known Shakespearean director Jack Lynn strongly believes that actors, directors, designers—indeed, everyone involved in a Shakespearean production—learn more by doing the Bard than producing a play by any other playwright. But there are even more reasons than that.

Seven Reasons Not to Attempt the Classics

1

. . . and All the Reasons Why We Should, Anyway

DALE LYLES

W e've all heard the reasons why it's not a good idea for your small, struggling theater to take on Shakespeare. The reasons, I think, boil down to seven specifics. Here they are—and here are all the reasons why you shouldn't pay any attention to them.

1. They are too hard to costume. ■ The clothing of the past is too elaborate to reproduce. There are too many pieces, no patterns available, and nobody knows how to make them. Costuming a Shakespearean show also is too expensive because of the cost of each costume and the size of the cast.

Well, no one says you have to do a show in its original period. Shakespeare is famous for being easy to reset into more amenable periods. (Make sure, though, that the period in which you reset it relates to the play. It wouldn't make sense to set the wild and woolly *Taming of the Shrew* in the cool, cerebral eighteenth century just because you have costumes left over from *DuBarry Was a Lady*.)

But many period plays can be transferred into distant settings. At the Newnan Community Theatre Company in Georgia, we did *The Comedy of Errors* in which all the characters wore gray sweatsuits. Not only did the twins look alike—*everyone* looked alike. Each character wore a differently colored face paint; the twins, of course, matched. The result was an extremely physical style of *commedia dell'arte* performance. Audiences howled at the comedy, didn't miss the doublets. [See page 33.]

If you can do it, the joys of period costuming usually outweigh the frustrations. There is something glorious about putting together a world that looks and feels different than yours. Even if you don't go for precise historical accuracy—and who can afford all that brocade and trim?—the experience is good to have, both for your costumers and your actors. Our *The Winter's Tale* was a soul-fulfilling experience for the entire company. What a thrill when the entire court appeared onstage in full Elizabethan regalia.

2. The sets are too complicated. ■ These plays call for multiple sets in architectural styles that are far too ornate for us. The time, talent, and budget required are all more than we can handle.

Obviously, the complaint cannot be true about Shakespeare, since his plays were written to be performed without sets at all. Maybe you're thinking of Feydeau's *A Flea in Her Ear*, with its Act I drawing room and its Act II sleazy hotel with staircases, cutaway rooms, and revolving beds? (And a return to the drawing room in Act III.)

If your group is like mine, you can devote your resources to either elaborate sets or elaborate costumes—or neither—but not both. Instead, focus on the costumes and cut back on the sets: a simple chair or a single window is often enough to define the space for an audience. The audience will always focus on the actors, so costumes are more important.

3. The language is too hard to deal with. ■ Tackling all those long sentences and strange words is just too daunting for an actor. And don't even talk about verse!

The truth is that there is no such thing as an actor who can't, only an actor who won't. If your actors have talent, then the rest of it is a learning process. But who will teach it? There are plenty of books on acting Shakespeare, as well as videotapes. Buy them, read them, practice them. Build on what you read—keeping in mind, however, what you know to be effective within your own group.

When we perform Shakespeare, I set aside a sizable chunk of rehearsal time for workshopping and learning how to "do" Shakespeare. The result is that we have never had a problem casting our

Shakespeares; for *The Winter's Tale*, I had more than forty people audition for the twenty or so slots because they were excited about the chance to perform these marvelous texts. They have discovered that the language is not your enemy; it is your best tool. And what an amazing tool it is!

4. Nobody knows or understands the production styles of past periods. ■ Our director and designers don't have a clue about how the plays of Shakespeare were staged. The scripts don't help either, without a floor plan in the back and stage directions in parentheses.

So who says you have to do it precisely as they did in Shakespeare's time? Discover it for yourself. Make it work for you. Make it work for your audiences. Research, learn, create. You want to do *The Taming of the Shrew* in the Wild West? Do it—after you determine that it can be done and that it will work, illuminating what the play has to say.

5. Our actors do not have the training to do these antiques. ■ Local actors cannot possibly measure up to the standards familiar to audiences through such Shakespearean movies as *Richard III*. They've never done these kinds of plays and wouldn't know how to begin.

Of course they know how to begin. They begin by reading the script, learning lines, fleshing out the character, exploring through rehearsal and endless experiment. How else would they begin? Who says you have to have been to Stratford or Juilliard to know how to begin these things?

As far as measuring up to Emma Thompson and Kenneth Branagh, who can? Most skilled professional actors can't. But that doesn't mean your production is not enjoyable or worthwhile. How many times have you had an audience member tell you that they had seen your show on Broadway and enjoyed yours so much more? Truthfully, do you think that your production was more polished than the professional Broadway production? Probably not, but if the audience enjoyed it, they enjoyed it. Besides, every show ought to stretch the company's members in some way; they will appreciate it.

6. These plays do not have the audience appeal that modern plays do. ■ Great works? No, they're too long, boring, obscure, elitist, and esoteric. They may be great to scholars, but not to our audiences. Our audiences would not come to see them and, if they did, they wouldn't be happy.

That has not been our experience at Newnan. If you pick an obscure, difficult Shakespearean play like *Titus Andronicus*, then you deserve what you get, I guess. But if you start out with the "safe picks" like *A Midsummer Night's Dream* or *The Comedy of Errors*, the audience will have as much fun with them as they would with any other well-produced script. Overheard in the parking lot after our production of *Twelfth Night*: "That was really funny. Who wrote that?" (That production, by the way, was done in a bare room, costumed in contemporary beach-resort attire, all in hand-painted muslin.)

7. These plays would be too much work and not enough fun. ■ With all these difficult problems, it's not worth our time and energy to tackle one of these great works. All we'd be doing is beating our heads against the wall for no good reason.

No one has ever dropped out of one of our Shakespeares because they weren't enjoying it. And always they ask, "What's the next one?" We've come to feel over the years that even if we don't achieve perfection, even if our *The Winter's Tale* is not the Royal Shakespeare Company's, we still will have climbed higher than if we had selected some safe but minor script.

Indeed, as time goes by, you'll find that your company has become more "athletic" with the exercise and will be less likely to tolerate second-rate scripts. We all have only so much time; why waste it doing bad stuff?

Get thee to thy library and read one of the Bard's words. Plan it. Create it. Do it.

Committing to the Classics | 2

What to Do If Your Public Isn't Familiar with Works by the Bard

DIANE CREWS

*H*ave you ever produced a Shakespearean play that was so well known you thought it would be a sure thing? A play that everyone should know, a classic? And then your audience didn't know it at all—and no one bought tickets for it?

I have found out, much to my chagrin, that "well known" to some of us does not mean the general public—that is, our audiences—will know. Many of the classic Shakespearean works are, in fact, not known to the majority of the public. Yes, they've heard of *Hamlet* and *Macbeth* and *Romeo and Juliet* and perhaps some of the others, but do they know *The Winter's Tale* or *Henry VI, Part 1* or *Antony and Cleopatra*?

I think we need to do something about that. What happened at York Little Theatre a few years ago—with non-Shakespearean productions, but with classics that the public *should* know—illustrates well, I think, why we need to take action.

Several Christmases ago, we needed a fund-raiser, and so produced what I thought was a perfect holiday show. The house held 250. The performance I attended had an audience of about sixty—maybe. Later that week, at a play-reading committee meeting, I expressed my disbelief at the public's lack of response. But it turned out that only one of eight members of my own committee had ever heard of the show, and none of them had ever seen it.

So a very strong production almost went unseen. The show? *Amahl and the Night Visitors.*

Everyone Doesn't Know

But even that experience did not prepare me for what happened next. A special production was switched from our studio space to our mainstage because we were certain that audience demand would necessitate the extra seating capacity. The royalties we had to pay were more than double our standard, but so, we felt, was the potential box office. Everyone would want to come to this.

As director, I had been asked to speak at several community functions about the production, and although I didn't think extra publicity was needed, I also knew you can never have too much.

My first stop was a monthly dinner meeting of a local CPA group. At the meal's end, while the pianist warmed up, I told the audience how pleased I was to be there, and how excited the theater was to be bringing this particular production to the community.

I assured them that they immediately would recognize the music they were about to hear. Out of curiosity, I asked those who had seen the show somewhere before to raise their hands. Out of close to 150 in the audience, there were only three hands in the air!

The show was *The Fantasticks.*

Self-fulfilling Prophecy

Wondering whether this was just a local problem, I began surveying other theaters. The same answers kept surfacing: "They will only come if it's just been made into a movie." "People don't know these titles." "People think these plays are dated."

Well, at least we've identified a problem we can do something about. It seems to me that it is our fault people don't know many of the Bard's works—and we are the ones who can change things.

It's the ultimate self-fulfilling prophecy: By not doing the classics, we cut off the most obvious avenue for their continuance in the hearts and minds of our theatergoing public.

Do you remember the first time you saw *The Merchant of Venice*? Or your first production of *The Comedy of Errors*? Do you go to see other productions of these plays when they are nearby? I do, and I know why: it's because I remember them. I have experienced them somewhere along the line, and I was hooked.

I'm not necessarily suggesting a whole season of Shakespeare's more obscure works—or even a whole season of any of his plays. I'd settle for one per season, and a commitment to a revival of that title every ten to fifteen years.

But of course, just doing them is not sufficient to ensure their survival either. We must do them well. Nothing can beat a good production of a great play. And we must advertise what to many has become an unknown title.

How? Find an angle. If you're mounting *Troilus and Cressida*, explain to your potential audience how the play's young lovers are, in a way, a kind of parody of the lovers in *Romeo and Juliet*, a far better-known play.

Making a Commitment

Pennsylvania's Lancaster Opera Workshop did its first production of *Amahl and the Night Visitors* nearly fifty years ago. The show was new then, and being done every Christmas season on television, so audiences were plentiful. But as years went by, interest waned and the public began to forget the story and lose interest.

What did the Opera Workshop do? Stop mounting the production and never do it again? No, they made a commitment to a classic theater work and continued *Amahl* as an annual event. The group ultimately chose to take the production on the road, and they now have a beautifully mounted touring show that goes into churches, schools, and other theaters. The demand is so great, they take bookings a year in advance.

Like the folks involved in that production, I fervently believe that if we do the great works of Shakespearean literature—the classics, whether they be well known or not—the audience will come, and come again.

DIRECTING THE SHAKESPEAREAN PLAY

While there is always a myriad of choices facing the director before embarking on any production, the choices confronting the director of a Shakespearean play can seem that much more daunting. Most of the plays are well known. They have been performed for centuries. Most everyone knows—or knows about—*Romeo and Juliet*, *Hamlet*, or *A Midsummer Night's Dream*. Many in our audiences have already seen productions of these plays, watched movies of them, or at least know the stories and are familiar with their plots.

Because the works are classic, they can be intimidating. Because they've been done so often and for so long, they can't be done by the numbers. They require rethinking, reinterpreting, reconstructing—even if you're thinking of doing the play in a traditional manner.

What, then, can a director do to make these plays new to an audience? Will setting the play in a different period or in a different place make it fresh? And how do you do that while maintaining the integrity of the work—and the interest of the audience, which might be expecting to see a classical production of a classic play?

Then there are the questions of language and length. Many directors believe that the strictures of iambic pentameter, the topical references, and the occasionally archaic language are barriers to a full understanding of the plays. So, too, might be the play's length. A director must confront the question of whether an audience today is willing or able to sit through a play that could be significantly longer than the traditional two or two-and-a-half hours.

Because the plays were written so long ago and because they are no longer protected by copyright law, the works of Shakespeare can be a blank slate to a director. You can make of them something intensely personal and show off your creativity and insight. While they offer immense challenges, they also offer wonderful opportunities.

"Well, At Least It's in English, You Know" | 3

You've decided that yes, you are going to mount a Shake-spearean production for your company. Where do you start? There's so much to think about—which play to choose, the style of the production, the period of the production, how to train your actors, their accents, the set design, the costumes, and so much more. What you need is a broad overview to get you started. Jack Lynn, a renowned Shakespearean director and teacher, offers an expansive look.

Tips on Producing Shakespeare

STEPHEN PEITHMAN

Whether you've done Shakespeare before, are considering doing so, or are shying away from it, you can learn a lot from Jack Lynn. Lynn was trained as an actor at the Royal Academy of Dramatic Art and has performed at the Royal Shakespeare Theatre, Stratford-upon-Avon, and other British and American theaters, in film and on television. He has directed for provincial and repertory companies in Great Britain, as well as for American companies, including the Pasadena Playhouse, where he was dean of the acting college for many years.

Why Shakespeare? Lynn's response is immediate.

"For actors, it's essential. It gives grounding to their other work; it provides a technique that makes doing modern plays so much easier. You learn how to breathe properly, how to phrase."

For theater companies, producing a Shakespeare play shows a commitment to their actors and to their audiences as well, he feels. We asked Lynn to share his almost fifty years of experience in several specific areas: play choice, setting, speaking of the lines, and directorial approaches.

Which Play?

If you or your company is new to Shakespeare, Lynn suggests starting with "something that people can really understand," he says. "I think *Julius Caesar* is a good choice. It's a political play, but it is also very straightforward. Then there are the comedies—*A Midsummer Night's Dream*, *Twelfth Night*, and *As You Like It*. Of the tragedies, I'd start with *Macbeth*. It goes right to the point, and it's the shortest. Start with these. Your audience needs to develop a gradual appreciation for the man's mind before it's ready for *Hamlet*."

Setting the Play

Shakespeare is done so often that many directors feel it necessary to set the play in a place and period other than the one originally intended [see Chapters 5 and 6]. Lynn isn't totally against such practice.

"One of the greatest productions of *The Merry Wives of Windsor* I ever saw was set in the 1950s. It worked because it was faithful to Shakespeare's intentions and characters. And, Lord knows, you have a lot of choices within the framework he provides. The famous letter scene in which the two wives meet was played in a hairdressing salon under the dryers. It was wonderful. But you cannot turn a comedy into a tragedy; you cannot change the intent of the characters or the story."

While Lynn feels that such changes may do no harm, he's also not convinced they're necessary. "There's no reason for a director to say, 'This play has been done so many times. How can I do it differently?'

"Just for a moment," he adds, "let's pretend there's a contract that says 'This play by William Shakespeare must be presented in Elizabethan style with no changes to the text.' Would every production be the same? No, because each would have a different cast, a different director, a different set and lighting design. They *couldn't* possibly be the same. That's why I think it's silly to approach any classic play, Shakespeare included, by asking 'How can I do this differently?' You must remember that a percentage of the audience will always be seeing the play for the first time. And, personally, I think that even regular theatergoers deserve a production that's being directed as if the entire audience were seeing it for the first time. Because they *are* seeing *your* production for the first time."

To Cut or Not to Cut

While he understands the need for cutting a Shakespearean text in some cases, Lynn believes that it must be done very carefully. He has harsh words for film director Franco Zeffirelli, who has brought *Romeo and Juliet*, *The Taming of the Shrew*, and *Hamlet* to the screen.

"Zeffirelli has no respect for the text of Shakespeare—he cuts and reorganizes shamefully. I thought Mel Gibson was marvelous as Hamlet, but Zeffirelli cut half of the 'rogue and peasant slave' soliloquy. What he doesn't understand is that there is a shape to Shakespeare. Gielgud says it exists in all great plays. It's called an 'arc,' referring to a curve of development within a play. Within the arc, there are scenes, and the scenes have an arc, as well. And each of the soliloquies and the great speeches also has an arc that guides you along. So for Zeffirelli to start Gibson halfway through the soliloquy violates the work itself."

Lynn worked with a private student who wants to direct *Hamlet* one day. "We went through the play, the two of us, scene by scene, analyzing it. And then we did it again, editing it, because he knows that in most commercial theaters—although it's a crime—you've *got* to cut it; audiences won't stand for four hours nowadays. And it's been very interesting, cutting so that we leave the verse intact. That is essential."

A Question of Language

Lynn and actor friend David Suchet were having a conversation about Shakespeare one day, and someone who overheard them said, "Well, I just don't understand the language." Suchet, well known now from public television performances, turned around and said, "You are so typical of people who come to see a Shakespearean play and you turn off too quickly. You don't listen and you don't pay attention. If you have patience and you listen, you will understand." Lynn agrees wholeheartedly.

"First of all," he says, "it's got to be a well-done production. Nothing is worse in trying to convert people to Shakespeare than a bad production. Bad Shakespeare can be a nightmare to people who have no idea of what they're going to see. But if they will just listen, then relationships between characters begin to happen, and eventually the idiom and the style of the language become clear to them. And suddenly they understand what is happening and what is being said. After all, there are modern English words that we don't know the meaning of, precisely, but when one of those words is used in the middle of a sentence in a modern play, we don't tune out, because we understand from the context of the sentence. And this is true of some of the archaic words in Shakespeare. I've had to say to more than one person in my life, 'Well, at least it's in *English*, you know.'"

And speaking of English, Lynn believes that trying to do an English accent only gets in the way for many American actors.

"As long as you're not going to speak New Yorkese, as long as you're speaking standard American, learn the lines as they're written. The lines are in [British] English, the 'melody' is in English, they're English phrases. Americans will accept it as English because of the phrasing."

Unless the actor is adept at accents and can do an appropriate one without thinking, dispense with the accent altogether, he advises. Otherwise, the actor will be thinking more about how to make the words sound than what the words mean.

"It's the same with Shakespearean verse," Lynn says. "You get these academic types coming in who say 'The stress must be on *that* word.' Well, that just gets in the way. What you *should* be telling the actor is to learn the lines letter-perfect—and their meaning. If you do that, the sense of it will carry the verse."

He's amazed at how many actors think that each end of a line of verse is the end of a sentence. "Look at the punctuation! If the last word in a line is connected by punctuation to the first word of the next line, speak it accordingly. It's called phrasing, and it's something that a good actor must learn to do—that and knowing the lines dead-perfect. Basically, if you learn the exact number of words in a speech and speak them well, you will get both the sense and the rhythm."

As a director, Lynn does correct people when they put an extra word into the verse, because that puts off the rhythm. "However, if the choice is between making an actor speak genuine English rhythms and holding him back, I'd rather see the character complete and emotionally true, speaking clearly and understandably."

Lynn's favorite example of this is the 1953 film version of *Julius Caesar*. "Finicky people said to me, 'Edmund O'Brien spoke his lines like an American!' And I said, 'I wouldn't have cared if he had sounded Australian. The performance and the phrasing were wonderful.' Gielgud once told me, 'You know, Jack, even in ancient Rome, there must have been varying dialects and accents.' And I think that's true. Everyone in a Shakespeare play should not sound exactly alike—*we* don't. Listen to the crowd scenes and the minor players in the film. You'll hear all kinds of accents. But it works."

Lynn does see value in renting film versions of Shakespeare.

Rent the MGM *Julius Caesar*, he says. "It may not be the most exciting Shakespearean film ever made, but to me it is the most authentic. The respect for the text is marvelous. And watch Gielgud's Cassius. I also think the Olivier *Richard III*—despite its cuts—contains magnificent performances by Gielgud and Ralph Richardson. I'm not overly happy about the Olivier *Hamlet*—he never was a very good Hamlet. But even when a great actor is bad, it's not bad bad, because the technique still comes through. And you can learn a lot."

Breathing Life into Shakespeare

Lynn does many workshops on Shakespearean performance, and finds the main problem is that "many actors simply don't know how to breathe properly. And breathing is the essence of all acting. That's why I say that if they do Shakespeare, they'll become better actors. You cannot get away without learning how to breathe properly, because Shakespearean sentences are much longer than in most modern plays, and the sense and the rhythm is carried with good breath control.

"One of the things I tell my Shakespeare students," he adds, "is that as you learn the lines and get used to the phrasing, mark where you are going to breathe. That way the breathing becomes part of the rehearsal process. With many actors, you tell them to breathe in and they heave up their shoulders and push their stomach in, instead of breathing through their diaphragm. You should be able to speak seven lines of Shakespearean verse—or any verse—on one breath."

Contrasts and Opposites

Contrast is the key to great productions of Shakespeare or any other playwright, Lynn believes.

"If you are directing a tragedy, look for all the comic moments you can find in it, because the contrast will serve you well. There are moments in *Hamlet* that are funny—really funny. And it makes the tragedy more horrendous. Likewise, if you are doing a comedy, look for the serious moments for the same reason. When I read a play for the first time, I go through it looking for places where I can ask the actors to play against the text—against the obviousness in the text. So that the thing has a dimension and can still be believable."

This leads Lynn to another observation. "You know what's missing today in the theater and film world? Charm. It's a dirty word. But charm is what gets an audience. How are you going to get an audience to react to you as an actor if you have no charm? Even a villain has charm—how else can he persuade people to do bad things? Remember Erich Von Stroheim— 'the man you love to hate'? When you see the charm in an evil person, it makes that person even more frightening. You sense the seduction. The person becomes more than a one-dimensional cardboard character. Even Hitler had charm, as evil as he was. He charmed a whole nation into following him."

Playing for contrasts—for the comic in the tragic, for the charm in the evil, for the dramatic in the comic—are all ways of helping an audience understand the Shakespearean plays. The technique also provides meat for the actor and director.

Final Thoughts

Ultimately, Lynn emphasizes that it is the playwright—Shakespeare or any other—who is the creator.

"Remember that the director and the actors are interpreters. I always look at a director as the conductor of an orchestra. The playwright has written the music. The director conducts and the actors are the instruments of the orchestra. And each characterization should have its own vocal rhythm, its own vocal colors. Even in a modern play, the audience should find the sound so comforting that it is a kind of music to them. The overall music helps each actor keep the rhythm of his individual characterization."

What sabotages Shakespearean productions all too often, says Lynn, is that the director and actors think of it as Holy Writ, instead of a living, breathing creation. Lighten up, he advises.

"The two basic requirements for work in the theater are a sense of humor and a sense of proportion. I've come across directors who have said, 'I have no sense of humor.' My basic reaction is, 'Then what the hell are you doing in theater?' "

Plumbing the Unknown Bottom | 4

As in all aspects of theater, we can learn best from those who have traveled the road before us. The director who has confronted the Shakespearean challenges again and again understands the pitfalls—and the benefits.

A Conversation with Barry Edelstein

IRIS DORBIAN

When Barry Edelstein was tapped by New York's Classic Stage Company to become its new artistic director, his ascension to the top rank of a theater devoted to innovative stagings of classics seemed long overdue. The thirty-four-year-old former Rhodes Scholar has amassed an impressive list of credits in classical theater (especially Shakespeare) throughout his accomplished career.

Starting with his four-year stint as assistant director/dramaturg to Joseph Papp at New York's Public Theater, Edelstein has directed more than half the plays in the Shakespeare canon at major theaters and drama schools around the country. However, it was his eyebrow-raising production of *The Merchant of Venice*, starring Ron Liebman at The New York Shakespeare Festival in 1995, that catapulted Edelstein into the spotlight.

In addition to his directing duties, Edelstein teaches Shakespeare at the Juilliard School, the Graduate Acting Program at NYU's Tisch School of the Arts, and The Public Theater's Shakespeare's Lab. He recently directed a new adaptation of Moliere's *The Misanthrope*, starring Tony Award–winner Roger

Rees and Uma Thurman, at CSC. Yet his heart and soul remain bound by his love of Shakespeare. In an interview, Edelstein discussed directing the Bard's timeless works.

sd: What is it about Shakespeare's plays that resonate so powerfully and personally for you?

EDELSTEIN: Well, a number of things. First of all, the sheer range of ideas and emotions that they encompass, the challenge that they represent, and the depth of them. I come back to given pieces of material again and again and continually find new things. There's a line in *As You Like It*: "It has an unknown bottom like the bay of Portugal." That's what I like about it. It's got unplumbable depth.

sd: When you're directing Shakespeare, what are the most important elements you consider?

EDELSTEIN: The text. The actors have to work through the material, thought by thought. It has to be specific; it can never be general. They have to think the ideas as the character thinks them. What you're always asking is, "Why am I using these words right now?"

sd: And those are elements that you like to impart to your students?

EDELSTEIN: Yes, and also to professional actors. If what I'm trying to say is, "The sun is coming up," I can say that in a million ways, but the way Horatio says it is: "But look the morn in russet mantle clad/Walks o'er the dew of high yon eastward hill." Why doesn't he just say the sun is coming up? One answer is because it's Shakespeare—that's how he writes. But that answer is only applicable in a graduate English literature class. In a rehearsal room, that's not a valid answer. You have to talk about why Horatio, the man, is speaking that way; that's the beginning of the exploration.

sd: Do you have a different approach when tackling modern plays as opposed to Shakespearean texts?

EDELSTEIN: No. I do the same work because a playwright is a playwright. It's the same process: What is the thought and why are you choosing this particular language to express that thought?

sd: What do you feel are the highs and lows of directing a Shakespearean play?

EDELSTEIN: The highs are definitely in being in the trenches in the rehearsal—just mixing it up with actors and designers in the rehearsal room. Also, I tremendously value the reading time with the script. I used to find the real low was when the show was well into its run in front of the audience and you just started feeling like a fifth wheel—completely irrelevant to the experience. But lately, when I've been doing runs of some more length, I've discovered that watching how the show changes over time is in fact a whole new thrill.

SD: You like seeing it evolve?

EDELSTEIN: Yes, I really do. When I was just starting out, I was a total control freak. I would get way out of joint if there was one gesture out of place. But recently I've really enjoyed how, night to night, it's extremely different—yet completely the same. I love that. I encourage actors who I work with to play around within the really clear limits of rhythm, form, and taste that we've agreed on in rehearsal. When you're working with someone like Roger Rees—the range of variation that he's capable of, within an absolutely rigorous commitment to the form we've set—is mind-boggling.

5 | *On Updating Shakespeare*

Probably the first question any director asks when preparing for a Shakespearean production is: Do I update? Of course, it's important to realize that *all* Shakespearean productions are modernized to at least some extent. That's because they are interpreted by a modern sensibility, a sensibility that is radically different from that of the sixteenth century.

But because the issues and insights—and, yes, even the humor—of a play by Shakespeare are so extraordinarily universal, the temptation is naturally to go beyond just imposing your modern sensibility. The lure, then, is to change radically the setting and period of the play—without, of course, violating the playwright's intent and the play's meaning.

The universality allows Shakespeare to be set in almost any conceivable circumstances. So, do you want to mount a "classic" production—that is, something that looks and feels traditionally Elizabethan—or a play set in a different time and/or place? Will setting the play in a different time and/or place make it resonate more with the audience? Will it open more doors into the play, give the audience another way of seeing it? On what basis do you choose a different time and/or place? How do you go about making those changes? The answers must begin with an understanding of why you might want to set your play differently.

The Choice Is Yours

The Berkeley Shakespeare Festival mounted a production of *The Taming of the Shrew* that included rap-singing and skinheads. The Ashland Shakespearean Festival in Oregon produced a Roaring Twenties version of *The Merry Wives of Windsor*. Across the continent, Falstaff underwent a gender shift in Washington, DC, where actress Pat Carroll played the hard-drinking, gluttonous, and womanizing comic character.

Back at the Berkeley festival, director Julian Lopez-Morillas staged *The Merry Wives* somewhere in 1903 Middle America. In other years and other places, directors have set *The Taming of the Shrew* in the Old West and *Measure for Measure* in a Central American police state. While there have been many instances of such directorial strategies with Shakespeare in the past twenty or thirty years, they do seem more frequent today. Why?

"I have an explanation for it, but it's not a very flattering one," Berkeley director Lopez-Morillas says. "I think there's an ongoing shift in American theater from a preoccupation with content to a preoccupation with style. The directorial concept is becoming the ruling fashion, so productions get judged not on how well they tell the story, but on how flashy and imaginative the setting is."

This is straightforward talk from one who seems to have bowed to the fashion he seems to dislike. However, Lopez-Morillas believes he has found the middle road in balancing content with style. "I'm all for good concept in Shakespeare if it illuminates the text, doesn't get in its way, and expands the theme," he says. What he objects to is reliance on gimmicks alone—"a substitute for thinking about the play and coming to grips with it."

A Certain Duty

The question most directors face in a Shakespearean production is how close to stick to the original. On the one hand, the Bard was writing for Elizabethan English theatergoers, and his language, allusions to contemporary life, and settings reflect this. While inextricably bound into any Shakespearean play, these matters can easily alienate modern American audiences. On the other hand, Shakespeare is a great writer not only because of his insight into the human condition, but also for the beauty of his language. How does one reduce the "alienating factors" while preserving what is great?

When Berkeley director Lopez-Morillas set his production of *The Merry Wives of Windsor* in 1903 Middle America, it was with the intention of creating a sense of familiarity for the audience. The kind of midwestern river town where he reset the play is, he believes, "a part of our national consciousness, even if we have no personal experience with it."

In the traditional Shakespearean production, the American audience must work its way through the Elizabethan setting, allusions, and language. In his production, Lopez-Morillas has eliminated references to the royal court and has changed *thee* and *thou* to *you*. Even though these changes seem minor—if one accepts the shift in setting—Lopez-Morillas seems compelled to justify them not by his earlier comments on accessibility, but by downplaying *The Merry Wives* itself. "It's a playful play about the middle class and, frankly, it's not a great piece of literature," he says. "It's entertainment. I don't think it's sacrilege to tamper with this play. It's not poetic or elevated in its own right, but with Shakespeare, you do have a certain duty to stay with the dialogue."

What the director of a Shakespearean play must decide, of course, is how much do you stay with the dialogue and how much do you "tamper" with the play. These are directorial decisions that you can't make with other playwrights whose works are not in the public domain, but they are choices you are forced to confront when you tackle the Bard.

The Play's the Thing 6

IVAN W. FULLER

*T*he prevalent question of the day for many community-theater directors regarding the staging of Shakespeare is: "Should we tamper with the time and place
settings of Shakespeare's texts?" It seems to me that
it would be virtually impossible to find an answer agreeable to
everybody. There always will be purists who firmly believe that
Shakespeare should be preserved intact on his Elizabethan
pedestal, and there always will be directors who can explain
why it is important to experiment with the staging of the Bard's
plays.

Since the question of "Should we?" will never be agree-
ably resolved, I'd therefore like to pose a new question. If we
acknowledge that many directors will continue to set Shakespeare's texts in non-Elizabethan settings, it follows that we
should investigate *why* they chose a particular setting for a
particular play.

In interviews with five directors, I asked them to discuss
which factors led them to choose the period they did for their
production and how they implemented those decisions.
Three directors were associated with the Stratford Shakespeare Festival in Ontario: David William, who directed a

modern-day version of *Troilus and Cressida* set in the Middle East; Peter Moss, who directed an Edwardian version of *Much Ado About Nothing*; and Richard Monette, who directed a production of *The Taming of the Shrew* set in 1950s Italy. I also talked with two university directors: Ronald Shields, of Bowling Green State University, regarding his production of *Twelfth Night* set in 1919; and Philip Kerr, of the University of Michigan, for his punk-rock version of *A Midsummer Night's Dream*.

All five directors were extremely helpful and articulate in discussing the rationale for their directorial choices. The results are summarized in the following six guiding values or criteria. These should be useful to any director evaluating the possibilities of a Shakespearean production.

1. The Text ■ The guiding value that was most often expressed was the text itself. All five directors claimed to derive their decisions from their interpretations of the text. In other words, the text "told" them how it could be adapted and how well it would work in different settings, at different times.

2. Accessibility ■ Several directors wanted to find a way to bridge the gap between the text and the audience. They wanted to make the text more accessible by placing the world of the play closer to the world of the audience. By doing so, they hoped that the audience would perhaps better comprehend what Shakespeare was trying to portray. The directors emphasized that this bridging had to be handled carefully so as to avoid patronizing the audience.

3. Issues ■ Closely related to bridging the gap was the criterion of shedding new light on an issue—social, political, religious, or ethical—that can be communicated through the text. The directors reasoned that such an issue might take on greater meaning and significance if it could be presented in such a way as to illustrate the parallel to the world of the audience.

4. Story ■ Many directors were guided by a desire to tell the story in such a way that the audience would not be confused. The large number of characters and tangled plots and subplots in many of Shakespeare's texts led these directors to believe that the audience needed help with the narrative elements, particularly character. For example, by setting the production in a period more familiar to the audience, costumes displaying social hierarchy would be more easily understood.

5. Education ■ A criterion unrelated to Shakespeare's texts, but very much a part of the productions by educational theater companies, was a pedagogical concern. Both Bowling Green's Ronald Shields and Michigan's Philip Kerr stated that the education of their cast and audience was of great importance; however, they seemed to differ in how that concern affected their staging choices. Kerr was concerned that his cast become comfortable with Shakespeare's text; his setting of *A Midsummer Night's Dream* in a punk-rock disco grew, he said, from his desire to use a world in which his cast would feel at ease—particularly important for his more inexperienced cast members.

6. Casting Considerations ■ The final criterion was expressed by Stratford's Peter Moss as an awareness of casting prior to making any staging decisions. While Kerr was concerned with inexperienced cast members, Moss considered who would be playing what role, then took that information and applied it to the choices he made about the world of the production. He did not want to place a performer in a world in which he or she was not physically well suited. He felt that his cast was more suited to an Edwardian setting than an Elizabethan one.

These six guiding factors appear to be general enough to be applied not only to Shakespearean texts, but also to any period play that raises the same concerns expressed here. They also indicate that discussing work practices is an important key to understanding why directors do what they do.

7 The Offbeat Bard

Six Companies Take Very Different Approaches to Shakespeare, Proving That All's Well That Ends Well

A *Stage Directions* reader, Mike Fisher, wrote to us that he had never directed Shakespeare at his high school, "mostly because of the limited connection that Shakespeare has for my audience and also because working with the Shakespearean text and high school actors is long and arduous."

However, he continued, "I hit upon an idea last spring for doing *Twelfth Night* set in 1978 in the Pacific Northwest, implying that the two factions represented loggers (Olivia) and environmentalists (Orsino). From there, the ideas took off: chain-saw duels, Elvis impersonators, and disco. The interest in doing the show soared."

His success prompted Fisher to suggest an article recounting similar experiences by other companies. So, we invited readers to share some of their own stories, and added to these some case histories of our own.

What we found was that "offbeat" to some people meant unusual costuming or settings, while to others it meant rewriting or cutting the originals to meet the needs of their players and audiences. Still others adopted policies aimed at trying to get back to the spirit, if not the letter, of the Elizabethan stage. All believed that their particular approach was both appropriate and faithful to Shakespeare's intentions.

To Cut or Not to Cut

The question of whether to perform Shakespeare's plays in their entirety or in edited versions seemed primarily a question of degree to the companies with whom we spoke.

The Shenandoah Shakespeare Express is a Virginia-based touring company that keeps cuts to a minimum.

"We cannot know precisely how long Shakespeare's plays lasted," says cofounder Ralph Cohen, "but the chorus in *Romeo and Juliet* promises 'two hours' traffic of our stage.' The Express strives to fulfill that promise with minimal pruning of text. We have found Shakespeare's plays can be performed in two hours through brisk pacing, no intermission, and a continuous flow of dramatic action. SSE audiences hear as much of Shakespeare's text in two hours as in many modern three-hour productions." Recently, the SSE hit the two-hour target without needing to cut *The Tempest* or *Twelfth Night*, and the SSE *Hamlet* used ninety percent of the First Quarto text.

The Cincinnati Shakespeare Festival takes the same approach, according to Artistic Director Jasson Minadakis. "There are no lines or characters cut," he says of his company's productions. "It's just blindingly fast."

Not surprisingly, the length of many of the plays and their seemingly difficult language was a concern mostly in high school and children's theater.

"Over the years, we have done and seen some wonderful cuttings and interpretations of Shakespeare's works," says teacher Cathy Archer, of Rutland, Vermont. "Among our library of cuttings is an *Othello* that incorporates a chorus that fills in the blanks made by the cutting. The chorus members are the Fates who weave the web that Iago creates. A cutting of *Love's Labour's Lost* focuses on the wooing of the princess, takes place in a corporate board room, and is staged as a soap opera. A series of short scenes from different plays are stitched together as pickup lines in a 1920s speakeasy. At a local high school Shakespeare festival, one group reset *The Taming of the Shrew* as *The Taming of the Brute*—Petruchio became Patricia and Kate became Nathaniel. The last speech was great when done by a guy."

Another vote for adaptations comes from Cathy A. Brookshire, artistic director (and often producer) of Shakespeare Live!, a pair of touring companies of high school students in Virginia. Brookshire

started out with twelve youngsters from three local high schools doing a thirty-minute "kinetic theater" version of *Macbeth* called *The
Witches Tale*, a piece written by Linda Burson.

"The next year we hired a high school English teacher to write a
one-hour adaptation of *Romeo and Juliet*, and things just went crazy
from there," she says. Sponsored by Performing and Visual Arts
Northwest, Shakespeare Live! now attracts young actors from six
counties. Recently, Brookshire directed *The Comedy of Errors* with a
company of students from five area public and private high schools.
They performed three shows a day, plus workshops, at each performance location.

Poetic license was at its greatest at The Royal Fairy Tale Theatre,
of Baldwinsville, New York. "We attempt to bring Shakespeare to life
by use of modern characterization and silly reference," explains
company founder Chrissy Clancy. She points to the use of the (rewritten) theme song from *Gilligan's Island* in her production of *The Tempest*. ("Well, hey, after all, it *was* a shipwreck!")

However, Clancy tries to maintain the Elizabethan language as
much as possible. "I strive to stay true to Will's stories and try not to
alter the actual plot line," she adds. "Of course, you haven't lived until you've seen Caliban exit on the line, 'What a thrice-double . . . .
donkey was I. Toodle-oo!' But on a warm summer's evening, with
the fresh, sweet smells drifting across the stage from our hay-bale
seating as you listen to the clear and true voices of the children
quoting Shakespeare, you know in your heart that the Bard would
be proud."

Exotic Locales and Costumes

While Mike Fisher experimented by resetting his production of
Twelfth Night in the Pacific Northwest, this is business as usual at the
Newnan Community Theatre Company, in Georgia, which has been
doing decidedly offbeat Shakespeare since 1978.

"In our production of *Twelfth Night*, the coast of Illyria became
a summer resort," explains Dale Lyles, the company's artistic director. "Everyone was in Ocean Pacific patterned shorts and shirts,
made of muslin and hand-painted with dye. Olivia began in a gray
sheath and switched to a rose prom dress. Malvolio wore gray
slacks and white shirt, black tie, and he carried an obnoxious black
clipboard, onto which he wrote all of Olivia's commands, and from
which he read her instructions. When his big change occurred, he
wore hightop sneakers laced all the way up his yellow knee socks,

yellow shorts, yellow tank top, and a yellow clipboard. Audiences howled."

In the company's *Pericles*, every scene, every locale had its own look, its own feel, Lyles says, including a "quasi-Victorian Tarsus in black/browns, a quasi-1790s Pentapolis in rose/whites, toga-ed Ephesus in blue/yellows, the whorehouse in 1940s Sicily, and the finale all in white. The effect heightened the audience's sense of panorama and epic. The Bawd, incidentally, was played by a man in drag."

The company decided to put on *The Comedy of Errors* as a stark contrast to recent period productions it had mounted. "The set was post modern ultramarine blue, with a single chrome-yellow trench running down the center—don't ask me why," Lyles says. "The entire cast wore gray sweatsuits and each wore a different color makeup on his or her face and hands; the twins had identical colors, of course. This worked very well for several reasons. First, in a play about identity, where the concern is how to make the confusion about the twins seem credible, the audience found itself not able to tell anyone apart at first glance. And yet, in a world where everyone had differently colored faces, it seemed perfectly natural to confuse two people with orange faces and two people with blue faces, even though, physically, they were nothing alike. Second, and this became clear to me as we headed into rehearsals, a painted face becomes a mask. It forced the actors to develop an extreme physical language well suited to the farce of the play. Very *commedia dell'arte*, very vaudeville. And very, very funny."

Newnan's resetting of Shakespeare is unusual only in that the company *prefers* to do things that way. Most other companies we heard from engage in the offbeat only on occasion. For example, California director Kim McCann set her Woodland Opera House production of *The Taming of the Shrew* in the Old West. The Cincinnati Shakespeare Festival presented *As You Like It* in a 1950s setting.

Both companies do a great deal of Shakespeare, usually in period settings. Anything different must support the play. As Cincinnati director R. Chris Reeder explains: "*As You Like It* is Shakespeare's pastoral comedy, meaning that it is representative of a 'golden age.' Since the decade of the 1950s is indicative of modern America's golden age, I chose to combine the two."

Back to Basics

On the other hand, a number of companies eschew anything but the basics.

"Our emphasis is on the actor, not on sets or costumes," says Cathy A. Brookshire, of Shakespeare Live!. "The actors wear logo tee shirts and blue jeans, and work barefoot. We have six boxes, built by a company member, that we use for 'sets' and to hold props and accessories. We perform in seventeenth-century English. The actors never leave the performance area and we double and triple roles, with actors changing character right in front of the audience."

Why the bare feet?

"We work hand-to-hand combat, daggers, and quarterstaffs," Brookshire explains. "When my actors are forced to take off their shoes, we have a lot less trouble with combat safety, and it makes them a lot more aware of the different spaces we have to work in."

While the use of contemporary clothing for staged Shakespeare might seem another gimmick, it actually has roots in Elizabethan England, as Jim Warren, of Virginia's SSE, points out. "Renaissance costumes may have been sumptuous, but they were certainly contemporary," he explains. "In other words, *Julius Caesar* was not performed in togas; actors would probably have added some 'Romanesque' elements to their Elizabethan clothing."

Following this precedent, SSE actors wear contemporary clothing, adding pieces designed to distinguish character, rank, and role. Likewise, Cincinnati Shakespeare Festival's production of *The Taming of the Shrew* had no costume designer. "Goodwill has really gotten to know us," artistic director Jasson Minadakis says. "We didn't pay more than $2 for anything. That includes the wedding dresses."

Back to the Future?

At some point, everything old is new again. In its emphasis on producing plays in the spirit of the Elizabethan stage, SSE lights the house as well as the stage.

"An Elizabethan actor could see his audience," explains the company's Ralph Cohen. "Shenandoah actors can see theirs. When actors see an audience, they can engage with an audience. Furthermore, in a universally lit venue, a spectator cannot avoid seeing other spectators in addition to the performance. The dual awareness of actor and audience makes for drama that plays to both fictional and real spaces. Leaving an audience in the dark can literally obscure this dynamic."

Doubling parts is another Elizabethan technique. As noted earlier, the Shakespeare Live! company doubles and triples roles. So does the Shenandoah Shakespeare Express. "Shakespeare's plays have as many as fifty roles, but Shakespeare's traveling company may have had fewer than fifteen actors," explains Jim Warren. "With a company of eleven men and women, the SSE frequently doubles parts, with one actor sometimes playing six roles in a single show. Watching actors play multiple roles, an audience can experience another aspect of Renaissance audienceship—the realization that actors are acting."

That realization is tied to another: While one might quarrel with some of the approaches described here, there is no doubt that to these practitioners Shakespeare is no museum piece, but rather a living, breathing thing.

8 | *Back to Basics?*

NEIL OFFEN

You want your Shakespearean production to look just like the play did back in the Bard's day? No fancy adaptations to a different culture, a different century, for you. You want to go back to the Bard's original, true style? Yes, but what exactly *is* that style?

"What most people today call 'Shakespearean,' the doublet-and-hose look, actually is usually a vague version of Renaissance," says David Hammond, artistic director of the PlayMakers Repertory Company in Chapel Hill, North Carolina. "And that look is actually a century or two *before* Shakespeare."

And the Bard's characters didn't speak "Elizabethan," adds Hammond, who has directed dozens of Shakespearean plays. "Instead, they speak iambic pentameter, a highly theatricalized language that no people anywhere ever spoke in the street," he points out. When people say they want to go back to the original, Hammond says, what they "really mean by original is what the Old Vic used and popularized in the 1930s. Sort of a vague, stagey Renaissance style."

Trying to recreate an "original" look is doubly difficult, he says, because the plays were all shot through with anachronisms.

"Take *Hamlet*, for instance. The play was written in the late sixteenth or early seventeenth century and tells a story set in the twelfth or thirteenth century, with people shooting off guns and cannons they couldn't have had, drinking English wassail in Denmark, and quoting the Bible and using the crucifix to ward off spirits in an uncivilized country that had not yet accepted Christianity. Yet the people were civilized enough to send their sons to school in Germany and on holiday to France."

The plays were packed with anachronisms because specificity of locale was not one of the Bard's concerns, Hammond notes. "What he probably had in mind was a sort of poetic visualization, free of the limiting characteristics of a strict time and place, but with enough detail to give his audiences a sense of the characters, their relations to each other, their positions in the world of the play, and their roles in the action of the story."

If the setting of your Shakespearean production does that, says Hammond, it really doesn't matter where or when you set it. It doesn't matter if it's "Elizabethan" or turn-of-the-century America or the Middle Empire in China. "You try to find a look that works," he says, "a look that helps the play speak to its audience. If all you've done is move it to another time, you've done nothing. If you do it without re-imagining the play, it's just like putting it in doublet and hose without understanding why."

When some critics complain and say you can't shift Shakespeare to other locales and times, Hammond says, "they are forgetting that that is exactly what Shakespeare himself did."

9 | *The Kindest Cut*

Another major choice confronting the director of a Shakespearean play is whether—and how much—to cut from the written text. Again, because the work of the Bard is in the public domain, this is not an option that occurs with most modern playwrights. But when dealing with the Bard, the question comes up, particularly because some of the plays can have running times of up to four hours.

As discussed previously, there are ways to trim the running time without necessarily cutting the text. Pacing can be a factor. But with works that are also replete with what are obscure references to today's audiences and sometimes archaic language, the question of whether to cut or not to cut must be met head on.

Practical Advice on When and How to Trim Shakespeare Down to Size

JAMES A. VAN LEISHOUT

For better or worse, most modern productions of Shakespeare are not presented whole. The reasons for cutting include time constraints, clarity, staging problems, and the personal preferences of the director.

To cut or not to cut—and what to cut? These, indeed, are the questions. While it's true that the Bard's plays probably were cut and rewritten for subsequent productions in his own lifetime, it's important to treat the text with respect. Cutting for the lowest common denominator may damage the play more than help it, and ruin the attempt to reach new audiences.

Good articulation and projection have done more to aid Shakespearean productions than all the editing ever accomplished, especially if the actors understand what they are saying and communicate that meaning to the audience. If the prologue to *Romeo and Juliet* is correct—and period references indicate it is—then most plays of Shakespeare's day ran about two hours long. A two- or two-and-a-half-hour Shakespearean production is still a workable goal today, achieved by picking up the pace and streamlining set changes. In "The Offbeat Bard" [see Chapter 7], Ralph Cohen, of the Shenandoah Shakespeare Express, explained how his company uses minimal pruning of text. "We have found Shakespeare's plays can be performed in two hours through brisk pacing, no intermission, and a continuous flow of dramatic action," he said. SSE audiences hear as much of Shakespeare's text in two hours as in many modern three-hour productions. The SSE hit the two-hour target without needing to cut *The Tempest* or *Twelfth Night*, and its *Hamlet* used ninety percent of the First Quarto text.

The first responsibility of a director is to honor the playwright's intentions; thus, using the entire Shakespeare text is almost always preferable in most cases. However, even Shakespeare scholars agree that some plays, such as *Love's Labour's Lost*, with its myriad of topical references, can benefit from careful pruning.

These few simple guidelines may help.

1. Have a clear understanding of why a line, scene, or character exists before cutting. ■ Whether it's topicality, repetition, or stage conventions and logistics, your understanding of the function of a scene, line, or character can aid in cutting. For instance, in the first scene between Titania and Oberon in *A Midsummer Night's Dream*, Titania cites "nine men's morris filling up with mud" as evidence of the effect his brawls have had on the weather. "Nine men's morris" refers to a popular game, a reference that is completely lost on contemporary audiences.

In *Romeo and Juliet*, the prince banishes Romeo for Tybalt's death. In the next scene, the nurse tells Juliet of the banishment, and in the very next scene the friar tells Romeo of the banishment. At Seattle Children's Theater, the director dealt with this repetition effectively by cutting the prince's scene, putting intermission just after the fights, and letting the next two scenes communicate the essentials to the audience. In contrast, the recent Baz Luhrmann film version cuts the scene with Juliet and the nurse without losing vital information.

Before cutting all repetitions, make sure the scene doesn't contain other information integral to character development or plot. [In this process, we recommend *Backwards & Forwards: A Technical Manual for Reading Plays*, by David Ball; published by Southern Illinois University Press; ISBN 0-8093-1110-0.]

Some scenes are simply devices to get more important characters onstage. In *Hamlet*, Act II, Scene 2, Rosencrantz and Guildenstern enter with the king and queen and report what everybody including the audience already knows—Hamlet is acting strange. The real point of the scene begins with Polonius's entrance. Modern lighting techniques or inventive staging can solve many of these problems without the unneeded lines.

Shakespeare's plays tend to climax in Act III. Act IV and the beginning of Act V are usually part of a long denouement, with a build toward a secondary climax at the end. These are good places for substantial cuts.

In *Macbeth*, Act IV, Scene 3, it takes 160 lines for Malcolm to test Macduff's loyalty. The doctor then enters to say the English king is delayed, and finally Ross enters to tell Macduff of the death of his family. The scene between Malcolm and Macduff can be cut at least in half, and the obscure reference to the divine right of kings and their healing hands can go.

In *Hamlet*, Polonius sends Reynaldo to spy on Laertes who has just left for school. While this shows the audience more of Polonius's character, it is not crucial information and merely assures that he is on stage when Ophelia enters to tell of Hamlet's odd behavior. One less actor is needed to play Reynaldo.

2. Be aware of emendations. ■ Emendations are conjectural corrections inserted in a Shakespearean text by an editor in an attempt to restore the original meaning. Unfortunately, the plays were often carelessly printed and there is no evidence that Shakespeare ever concerned himself with seeing them accurately reproduced. As a result there are a large number of errors in the early editions of his plays that scholars through the centuries have struggled to correct. For eighteen of the plays, as many as four quartos exist in addition to the First Folio. *Hamlet*, for example, has more than two hundred lines in the Second Quarto that do not appear in the First Folio. The folio has about eighty-five lines that don't appear in the quarto printing. Fearing to leave one hallowed word out, editors have included them all. For the other seventeen plays, the First Folio (published soon after Shakespeare's death) is the sole source. But some scholars still quibble over obscure word usage and scene order.

You can use a replica of the First Folio as a guide to cut through all the additions, or check the Folger edition of the plays, which identifies which lines are exclusive to which source. This greatly simplifies the process of identifying emendations. Often the various lines from either the quarto or the folio are unneeded.

3. Examine which cuts other directors may have done. ■ Film cuts are the most readily available and the time constraints of film (with the occasional exception, such as Kenneth Branagh's *Hamlet*) almost always demand cuts. Viewing these can give you the courage to make your cuts. However, don't get caught up in that particular director's concept.

4. Question why scenes are in a given order. ■ Any temptation to move all the court scenes in *As You Like It* together, for example, should be carefully reconsidered. The court scenes are rather dark and the interspersing of the forest scenes avoids delaying the funnier comic elements, which is what captivates audiences. Understanding Elizabethan stagecraft offers clues as to why a scene or speech can be moved. Stages were approximately forty feet wide then, which allowed quick transitions of scenes and speeches such as "To be or not to be" to stand alone.

5. Don't cut famous lines. ■ If you cut famous lines, you risk upsetting audience members. At the very least, the evidence of your tinkering will be obvious to many. If you are unsure which lines are famous, the Folger editions list most of them in the back of their scripts. Or simply look through *Bartlett's Familiar Quotations*, which lists the famous quotes play by play.

6. When finished, check to see what you have created. ■ Each fifteen lines represents about two minutes of stage time. If you are calculating for a specific length, did you allow time for fight scenes, songs, dances, comic bits, etc.?

A continuity check makes sure actors have time to get off stage and back on for the next scene and that audiences are going to accept passages of time. Again, creative staging can solve some of those problems, but be aware of them. Ask yourself if the play is still by Shakespeare. If you have cut or stretched the script beyond the limits of authorship, you may want to retitle or use a subtitle like "based on the play by William Shakespeare."

7. Remember, Shakespeare wrote to please his audiences, not critics. ■ While some purists and your high school English teacher may hate your two-hour *Much Ado About Nothing*, your audiences and box office may thank you profusely. Keep in mind, however, that a well-directed, well-acted, three-hour *King Lear* will be more exciting than a poorly done two-hour version. A short script is no guarantee of success, but it can definitely help.

10 | *When All Hell Breaks Loose*

If you're used to staging plays where the greatest violence is verbal, then directing Shakespeare—particularly the tragedies and history plays—offers a unique challenge. The plays are full of violent combat, and the Shakespearean director must know how to make that large-scale violence believable to an audience that has been weaned on hyper-realistic filmic clashes. (Knowing how to fight is also extraordinarily important for the Shakespearean actor; in Part III, we look at what the actor must do.)

Advice on How to Stage Melees, Brawls, and Other Big Fights

BRUCE LECURE

*I*t's one thing to choreograph a fight between two actors. But what about a melee, which the dictionary defines as "a noisy, confused fight or hand-to-hand struggle among a number of people"? What techniques do you use when all hell breaks loose?

Clearly, a noisy, confused fight is rife with hazards, so we asked a number of stage-combat experts their advice. Their methods differ, but all agree that to create an unchoreographed illusion of vicious, uncontrollable violence and still keep the actors safe, several factors must be addressed. These include various choreographic approaches, the number of actors, their skill level, the space, and the amount of rehearsal time.

Different Approaches

Fight directors prepare for a melee in different ways. Joseph Martinez, a fight master in The Society of American Fight Directors and a professor at Virginia's Washington and Lee University, does a great deal of prechoreography before he walks into that first fight rehearsal. He maps out the fight completely by using an intricate movement diagram, much as a dance choreographer might. Using one piece of colored tracing paper for each section of the melee, Martinez prefers to see the whole fight laid out in front of him.

Working in exactly the opposite way is David Leong, a fight master in The Society of American Fight Directors and chairman of the theater department at Virginia Commonwealth University. He plans the overall look of the fight, a few specialty moves, and perhaps the end of the fight prior to his first fight rehearsal, then constructs the entire fight improvisationally with his actors. He coaches them through their characters' thoughts and impulses moment-by-moment, their emotional through-lines, and helps them construct each part of the melee organically.

Drew Fracher's method of working on a melee lies somewhere between these two styles. President of The Society of American Fight Directors as well as a fight master, Fracher works out his movement patterns and plans certain moves/combinations that speak to the style of the fight, but also leaves room for more skilled actor/combatants to give choreographic input.

All three fight masters enjoy using a more stylized approach to a battle royal when it fits the conceptual world chosen by the director. A slow-motion fight or a combination between slow motion and regular speed can be an exciting choice for a group fight. Clearly, it is very important to work closely with the lighting and sound designers when considering a stylized approach to a battle.

Variations on a Theme

One widely used technique in staging a melee is to choreograph the whole fight to counts, as a dance choreographer might employ to construct a dance. In other words, the fight director assigns each part of each move by each fighter a specific length of time through the use of numbers, so each fight in a battle can be planned to begin and end at a specific time and space. For example, on Count 22, one actor in Group A might lunge with his sword at his partner, while another actor in Group B might be reacting to the pain delivered during Count 20, while a third actor in Group C might be lying on the ground, dying, and so on.

This manipulation of time in a melee is very important to help maintain safety on stage. The technique always is practiced in slow motion so that actors can memorize each movement before moving on to the next one. Counts help keep actors from fighting at different speeds and allow for different sections of a battle to safely interact with each other. A fight director usually will count out loud at a consistently slow rhythm or clap his hands to supply the beat. Using a metronome also can provide the consistent rhythmic base.

The use of counts also makes for more efficient use of rehearsal time. The fight director can begin a rehearsal of a battle at Count 42, for example, and each fighter will know exactly where to begin. (To be this familiar with the counts, the actors will need lots of rehearsal time.)

Martinez uses another unusual technique early in the rehearsal process—he blindfolds one combatant in each grouping. The blindfolded actor rehearses the fight in slow motion with a partner who is not blindfolded. This technique helps expand the sensory awareness of the character who is fighting, as well as forcing the blindfolded actor to be acutely aware of others on stage. Of course, this is only to be used as a rehearsal technique and never employed on stage during the actual violence in the script.

Martinez often videotapes the rehearsals and shows the battles to his cast. Thus, his actors literally see their mistakes and how to better incorporate the fight director's notes. Martinez also likes to watch the fight "with his ears." The sound of the battle, he says, needs to be designed as well. He often uses a loud or sharp sound to cue a visual action. "Sound sets up sight," he notes. "We need to communicate to our audiences through all their senses."

Fracher likes to focus on rehearsing with all characters on stage during a fight, both fighters and nonfighters. The reactions of the characters watching the Hamlet/Laertes fight is just as important a part of telling the story of the fight as the fight itself, he points out. All characters on stage need to help tell the story of any fight, especially the melee.

Telling the Story

Any stage combat scene, whether a two-person fight or a battle involving a group of fighters, needs to tell a story. And the story of the fight needs to advance the story of the entire play, say our experts.

"The fight itself has its own quality that adds to the dramatic quality of the entire piece," Martinez points out. "In a melee, the outcome of the fight is less important than a two-person fight. Characters need to be developed but less so. The most important issue is why they are fighting."

In any fight, safety is the most important factor. The director must make sure there is sufficient room on the set for the fight, as well as make sure no set piece or prop will accidentally cause injury to the actors.

This problem increases exponentially with a large-scale battle. The more actors fighting on stage, the greater chance for accidents. A fight director must not place too many fighters on stage during a melee. Give your actor/combatants plenty of room in which to work, and a clear view of the stage, so that a fighter does not injure another whom he can't see. Fracher puts it this way: "Each fighter needs to know exactly where everyone else is at all times. If one group gets out of their fighting area, a domino effect begins to happen. One fight moves into another fight, into another fight, etc." Once that happens, the careful choreography falls apart.

Often, fight directors choose to designate specific stage areas for each group of fighters. Some fight directors mark these with tape on the floor of the rehearsal room and/or on the set (only for the first rehearsal on stage). Other fight directors, like Martinez, choose not to use tape, but rather choreograph to fit the allotted space on the set. They prefer that their actors focus on their partners rather than a piece of tape on the floor.

Regardless of your style and technique, the safety of your performers should always be your number-one concern.

Varying Skill Levels

One of the unique challenges of directing a battle is dealing with the different skill levels of the actors, says Fracher. "If you don't have skills, you die quick!"

Since time is always at a scarce premium in the rehearsal process, a good fight director must immediately assess the skill level of his actors. (If you are lucky, some of your actors may have received combat training or may even be certified as an "actor/combatant" by The Society of American Fight Directors.)

Leong solves the skill-level problem by teaching his actors various contact/noncontact moves through "slow-motion contact improv" at the first fight rehearsal. Since he develops most contemporary fights through improvisation, at the conclusion of this first contact improv he is much more knowledgeable about the actors' abilities and can guide their improv choices more effectively. Martinez, having choreographed the fight on paper first, teaches the easiest and the hardest moves in the fight to the entire group of fighters during the first rehearsal. After this evaluation, he knows how much of his preplanned choreography needs to be adjusted.

After assessing the actors' skills, some fight directors divide their choreography into primary, secondary, and background fights. They place their most experienced actor/combatants in the primary fight, the less experienced in the secondary fights, and the least accomplished fighters in the background.

It is always wise to parcel out the fighting techniques based on the skill level of the actors. Give the flashy, more difficult moves to your primary and perhaps your secondary fighters. Give the background fighters simple skills they can repeat over and over during the fight (for example, struggling or grappling moves). Remind all fighters that they must always be in control of their bodies but need to "act" like they are out of control. The key to achieving this, most fight directors feel, is by working with your actors to help them maintain their balance. They need to keep their center of gravity low so their acting abilities can safely sell the illusion of a body out of control. The audience must sense that the characters' bodies are out of control, but the actors must not.

While a fine actor may be a natural for the show's lead, he's not necessarily the best fighter. The actor playing Macbeth may sound convincing but be scared to swing a sword. In this case, the experts say, it is often wise to cast a "ringer" or a very experienced fighter as Young Seward and/or Macduff so the experienced fighter can help make the lead actor look good.

When Time Is Limited

There never seems to be enough time to rehearse, especially for the fights. The most dangerous part of a play often is given the least amount of rehearsal time. The experts concur that many times this is the fight director's greatest challenge.

Most fight directors today work with this formula: Each five seconds of a staged fight requires one hour of rehearsal time prior to the first dress. Even so, a fight director should take a close look at the total amount of rehearsal time allotted and then choreograph the fight accordingly. Trying to direct a very complex fight with little rehearsal time is a formula for disaster. Begin the fight rehearsals as soon as possible, say the experts. Don't delay them until the end of the rehearsal period.

Also remember that a sixty-second battle is a very long fight in stage terms. Don't try to choreograph too much. Fracher points out that less is more. "A fight should only last as long as it needs to in order to tell the story, not a second longer," he says.

Directing the Focus

In a battle, as with any fight, directing the audience's eye is extremely important. An unfocused scene will confuse the audience and not tell the story of the fight or advance the play's action. The fight director must guide the audience's eye, moment by moment.

Our consultants say this can be done in several ways. The position on stage of a particular fight within a battle can help draw the focus of the audience. When you have many people moving on stage, a fight staged downstage center will draw the audience's eye more effectively than one upstage right. A fight taking place on a higher level often will make it a stronger acting area on the stage. Obviously, then, a fight director must analyze the set in terms of the strongest and weakest areas for drawing focus.

A sharp movement on stage also will draw the audience's focus. A quick lateral or diagonal movement during a battle definitely calls attention to itself.

Leong considers this his number-one priority. When he is stuck while choreographing his actors, he asks the question: What would the audience least expect at this moment? This gives him an action that provides both surprise and energy to the scene.

It's true that the stage already is charged with a great deal of energy when a group of people are fighting. But it's also true that proper preparation and an emphasis on storytelling and safety can make Shakespearean combat an exciting event for an audience to experience. It also can add to the dramatic quality of the entire piece.

11 | The Bard on a Budget

You've listened to Jack Lynn and Barry Edelstein, acclaimed Shakespearean directors who have worked in renowned theaters from coast to coast and abroad. You've decided where and in what period you are going to set your Shakespeare. You've decided on what to cut and how long your production will run. But, you say, what does the experience of directors like Lynn and Edelstein and others like them have to do with my situation? I don't have endless resources to spend on costumes and hiring marvelously trained actors. I don't work in an ideal situation. My resources and budget are limited; how do I put on a work by the Bard with those constraints?

The advice given by Lynn and Edelstein is advice that should be valuable to all theaters, at all levels. But there are, of course, questions that are specific to limited budgets. There are solutions, too.

Shakespeare in the Small

LINDSAY PRICE

These days, Shakespeare frequently is very large. Large casts. Large costumes. Large sets. Large budgets. In Shakespeare's day, the plays weren't performed with twenty to thirty actors, but rather with a small cast who wore stock costumes and used recycled set pieces.

My partner Craig Mason and I decided to perform a little experiment with another pair of actors, Todd Espeland and Allison Williams, who comprise the Florida-based company Commedia Zuppa. We would block, rehearse, and perform Shakespeare's *The Tempest* in five days. Why? To prove that Shakespeare can be done—and done well—on a small budget and to prove that there are new ways to approach the Bard.

The two companies couldn't be farther apart. Theatrefolk is a text-based company with a healthy Shakespearean background. We have studied, analyzed, performed, taught, and adapted a number of Shakespeare's plays. Commedia Zuppa, on the other hand, has an extensive physical-theater background. They are accomplished mask-makers who spend their time teaching and performing *commedia dell'arte* and stage combat. We knew that our different backgrounds would make for an exciting workshop. What follows is a day-by-day account of how we spent our week.

Monday—The First Rehearsal

Everyone arrives this morning with scripts in hand, knowing exactly what characters they will play. Since *The Tempest* has twenty-four–plus characters and we only have four actors, some edits have to be made. I've edited the script down to an hour and a half to make it feasible for four actors to move from character to character without any glitches.

Preparation is the key to a project like this. Months before this first rehearsal, a number of decisions were made and tasks were divvied up. I am the designated director and have come today with a blocking prototype for the show. Craig is playing Prospero, Stephano, Gonzalo, and Sebastian, and he knows most of his lines already. Since the show will take place in Florida, Todd and Allison take care of all the local work—such as booking rehearsal space and publicity. They have also taken care of the many masks we will use for the different characters. Even though a lot of work has already gone on, there is still so much to do! A bonus for the project is that there will be an article with pictures in the local paper later on in the week.

Tuesday—Blocking Like Crazy!

Our plan is to have the play blocked by the end of today and we're almost there. All we have left are a couple of flashy sections such as the storm at the beginning and some clown work among Stephano, Caliban, and Trinculo. We know that changes will be made, but it feels good to have some groundwork finished.

The four of us work well together. The piece is very much a collaboration: each of us has specific talents that we are lending to the show. However, we realize the importance of a decisionmaker. It saves time when all of us want a scene to go in a different way.

Wednesday—Fighting Panic

Today has been completely panic-stricken. And we had been doing so well. This has less to do with the actual acting and more to do with everything else that needs to be done. We spent a lot of time away from the rehearsal hall. Costumes have to be dyed. Prospero is without a staff. Masks need Velcro. It's the bits and pieces that are eating into our time. We're trying not to fall into the trap of getting more lights, more music, more stuff! It's a hard lesson to learn.

Thursday—The First Run-Through

Today is the day we put it all together and see what we have. Everyone is off book. There are still a number of holes, but the shape of the production is definitely there. We're finally clueing into the fact that this is a crazy idea. But that is what makes the process so exciting! We are throwing ourselves into it, without a real notion of failure. We have jumped without a net.

I think at this point, we're more scared of performing to a crowd of one rather than the production itself. However, the article appeared in the paper today, and it looks fantastic.

Friday—Will It Work?

We nix the idea of a full day of rehearsal. We're going to do a run-through in the morning and leave the rest of the day to rest. It's hard to do, but totally necessary. We've been rehearsing morning, noon, and night. We all know that a breaking point is close. On the other hand, we are so close to accomplishing what we set out to do. All that remains now is the performing.

Postmortem—It Worked!

The first show was all there, a little shaky, but our hard work paid off. It felt wonderful! We had an extensive post-show talk with the audience and used their feedback in the next show. They couldn't believe we started rehearsals on Monday. Each show got better and better and, in the end, we believe that the exercise was a complete success.

This is a fascinating exercise. It's such a learning process. You learn how well you work with others, how to defuse conflict, how well you can think on your feet. All are valuable tools to the working actor. It was also incredibly scary, which is a good thing to do every once in a while.

Do you need waking up? Get a group together and perform Small-time Shakespeare. You never know where it might lead. All four of us in *The Tempest* agree that the show is well on its way to a full-scale production. We can't wait to perform it again! Where will your show lead?

Small-Time Shakespeare

12

Six Rules to Follow When Working on a Budget

1. Know with whom you are working. ■ Know the people and what they are capable of—and what they can't do, as well. Know how to defuse conflict between the personalities.

2. Be sure to edit. ■ If you don't, you'll lose your mind with the time it takes to block all the scenes and memorize all the lines.

3. Keep it small. ■ Shakespeare did it with a small cast and so can you. Double the roles—or triple them if you have to.

4. Be prepared. ■ Always, always have a game plan before you start rehearsals. Decide on doing it a certain way and stick to that decision.

5. Have a Shakespearean expert on hand, or have access to one. ■ Make sure someone knows what all of the words mean in twentieth-century lingo.

6. Have a deadline. ■ Nothing makes you work harder than knowing the first show is around the corner.

ACTING THE SHAKESPEAREAN PLAY

*P*erforming Shakespeare is not the same as performing the works of any other playwright. For one, there are so many frames of reference against which a performance might be judged. You're doing *Hamlet*? Your audience might have memories of the Laurence Olivier *Hamlet* or the Mel Gibson one in films, and may have seen Richard Burton or Nicol Williamson or Ralph Fiennes on stage. How will your *Romeo and Juliet* compare to the one people saw at the Oregon Shakespeare Festival or any of the many movie versions?

Then, of course, there is the question of the language. As director Jack Lynn noted earlier, the texts *are* in English, but the words and the rhythms can feel unfamiliar to American tongues and ears. Iambic pentameter can feel unnatural. The meaning of the words and the references can be obscure, stripping them of the necessary expressive significance an actor needs. Further, Shakespearean plays demand specific Shakespearean movements, and many of the plays require physical actions not generally found in other more modern works.

Yet Shakespeare, in addition to being a playwright, was,

of course, an actor as well, and the roles he wrote are wonderful vehicles for those up to the challenges.

In Shakespearean times, women were not allowed to be actors, so all the female roles were played by preadolescent boys. To perform their roles, the boys were given extensive training in singing, dancing, music, memorization, weaponry, and other aspects of acting. Today, Shakespearean actors need to be masters of all those qualities. It may be difficult, but to master Shakespeare is also among an actor's most rewarding accomplishments.

Surmounting the Challenge

13

What Can an Actor Do?

JULIAN LOPEZ-MORILLAS

As directors of recent productions of Shakespeare channel their energies into creating arresting visuals and contemporary historic parallels, more and more actors and actresses are left grappling with the text on their own. Some theaters have a dramaturg, or even a voice coach or text specialist, on board who can help the actor when problems arise. But all too often, the performers are left not only to flounder with unfamiliar language, but also with a director who has neither the time nor the expertise to offer help. Under such impossible circumstances, an actor has no other viable option but to develop a personal approach that works and is dependent on no one. He or she must know how to handle verse and dissect the text, and do it with uncommon ease and skill.

Obviously, a top-notch conservatory or advanced drama training is a good place to get this kind of discipline. But if you can't afford that kind of commitment, then you must acquire the techniques on your own. My advice: read extensively. Get used to reciting poetry aloud. This will enable you to gain an appreciation for the way a good poet mixes sense, sound, rhythm, and imagery for maximum effectiveness in the fewest words. Read good books on Shakespeare's verse, such as Cicely Berry's *The Actor and His Text* and Delbert Spain's *Shakespeare Sounded Soundly.* They are terrific starters.

Learn to break down a line, a speech, and an entire character within the context of the language. Pore over books covering the history of the Renaissance. People thought very differently then from the way we think today: Shakespeare's plays mirror that time-specific perspective.

Get a solid edition of the play and use the notes. Editions like New Cambridge, New Penguin, and Arden are particularly useful, with comprehensive notes that help the actor deal with the language and clarify the meaning. The only way an actor can really hone into his or her role is by undertaking this type of text preparation.

Directors need to pay as much or more attention to the content of the play as they do to the style. Actors, for their part, must learn to do their own work on the text in order to make it clear, graceful, and above all, comprehensible. What an audience can't understand, it can't enjoy. A Shakespeare play produced in the year 2000 can be absolutely original and thought-provoking—even if it is set in traditional Renaissance dress and not the modern garb (complete with esoteric concepts) that some directors favor.

It is the freshness of the ideas that a company brings to the work—and their ability, through exploration, insight, and understanding of human nature, to realize their vision—that makes a play involving and vital. [See also director Jack Lynn's comments in Chapter 3.]

Move Like an Elizabethan | 14

For an actor playing Shakespeare, there is so much focus put on the language—as well as the related issues of accents, pacing, versifying, and projection—that sometimes the more physical activities receive short shrift. But mastering the correct movements is essential to creating believable Shakespearean characters.

Sitting, Standing, Gesturing, and Bowing As If to the Manner Born

BRUCE LECURE

*I*f your Shakespearean play will be set in the Elizabethan period, the question naturally arises: How can modern actors wear Elizabethan clothes and display the precise manners and etiquette of sixteenth-century England? How do you move with the grace and pride of a proper Elizabethan nobleman?

To be believable, actors must sit properly, stand accurately, gesture correctly, and bow to the queen herself with the precision necessary to survive in Elizabeth's strict world. Each performer should look as if born and bred to this environment. Otherwise, the play may have the forced look of modern actors moving and acting realistically, but dressed in very stiff and unforgiving period clothes.

The solution lies in the elements of dance, for the nobility during Elizabeth's time were taught by dance masters from the time they could walk how to sit, stand, walk, move, gesture, and bow. Here's how dance movement can achieve that "Elizabethan look," if practiced and mastered long before the costumes are worn at first dress rehearsal.

The Proper Stance

The Elizabethan period has a very "horizontal" feel. The costumes were wide and expansive, containing a great deal of padding and starch. An upper-class Elizabethan gentleman stood straight and tall in a wide second or slight fourth dance position (see the accompanying diagram) with his feet naturally turned out. He often rested his closed fist(s) on his waist as he looked out to the horizon.

The Elizabethan woman stood in either a first, third, or small fourth position. Her corset also demanded that she stand very lengthened and tall. The costume didn't allow her arms to fall by her side; rather, they were held so that there was "air under her armpits." Her hands often rested with the "heel" of her palms gently touching the wide skirt or with her right hand resting in the palm of her left. Her gaze didn't allow for a great deal of direct eye contact, as was customary for the men.

The Proper Walk

Both men and women during the Elizabethan period walked in straight lines and turned the entire body when changing directions or responding to a direct address (the ruff around the neck restricted head movement). An actor portraying an Elizabethan man takes large, strong steps; the steps of a woman are quite small, slightly larger than the length of her foot.

To wear the costume properly, the Elizabethan woman was required to glide when walking. There is no up-and-down movement; instead, the head "draws" a straight, horizontal line as the body walks across the room. The feet should not be visible under the dress as the body appears to float gracefully in space.

When walking together, the man may offer the woman the inside of his forearm or place his arm out (again, on a horizontal plane) for

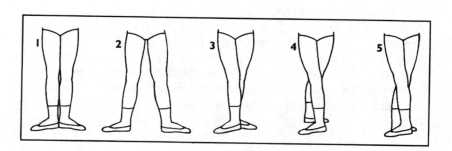

the female to rest her hand as they walk. Also, during rehearsal be sure to keep a good deal of distance between the two actors because the width of the costumes will require it on stage.

The Proper Sit

In addition to a woman's costume bulk and inflexibility, there might be a train. Trains need to be managed carefully to avoid the embarrassing trip or stumble on stage.

When sitting, approach the chair from behind at a forty-five-degree angle. You need to catch the chair out of your peripheral vision as you approach it. When your feet are in front of the chair, turn your whole body to the front, which will wrap the train around your feet, making it easier to control when choosing to stand and move again. Be sure to sit on the front half of the chair rather than against the back as we do today. Due to the point of the corset, the woman's feet were placed in an open second position. The action of sitting (for both men and women) needs to be smooth and controlled. Do not plop in the chair or reach for it as you sit. Sit yourself with a great deal of grace and ease. The male sits with his feet in a slight fourth position on the front half of the chair, with the same feeling of strength he exudes while standing.

The Proper Gesture

The gestures of the Elizabethan man, in keeping with his movements, were strong and executed on a strictly vertical or horizontal plane. Gestures for the woman were softer than the man's, but still on the same vertical or horizontal plane. In other words, avoid curves in your movement and gesturing. Be sure to also keep some "air under the armpits" for each gesture, as required by the costume constriction.

The Proper Greeting

Men greeted men of a similar rank by grasping each other's forearm. There was no shaking hands as we do today. If the men were very familiar with each other, they might choose to grasp both forearms—again, no shaking. Men might greet men or women with a slight inclination of the head and a slight opening of the torso to the other person. Men and women could greet each other by grasping both forearms and putting cheek to cheek on one side of the face or both. (A definite kiss is not required, but rather a simple touching of cheeks.)

The Elizabethan woman also might place one hand (or both) to her bosom as a sign of respect as she greets another. A man or woman would greet a superior (such as Elizabeth herself) by kneeling on the right with a lowered head. You might "kiss" the hand of superiors by taking their hand in your right as you kneel, placing the back of their hand to your forehead. You would never touch your lips to their hand (that is, actually kiss the hand), to avoid spreading any bodily fluids from the nose or mouth to the superior person. Be sure to rise and step away from this greeting in the opposite direction than you approached. Standing straight up at the end of such a greeting would bring you face to face with your superior—an insult by Elizabethan standards.

The Proper Bow

In a more formal situation (such as an audience with the queen, being introduced into a room, or asking someone to dance), a bow is a necessary act of respect. For the Elizabethan man, a leg (usually the right) moves forward into a slight fourth position with the weight evenly balanced on both feet. From this stationary position, he bends both knees (in dance terms, a *plié*) slowly and smoothly. His upper body bends forward slightly from the hip socket as he plies. The depth of the bow depends on the amount of respect he wishes to show to the other person: the more respect, the deeper the bow. He slightly opens his arms/palms as he pliés. Men slowly lower their eyes as they bend their knees, and then raise their eyes and straighten their legs at the bow's conclusion. If the actor is wearing a hat, he removes it with his right hand at the beginning of the bow, and replaces it or holds it by the side of his body at the end.

The proper Elizabethan woman bows by bringing her feet together in a first position and bending her knees in the same manner as the man. However, the upper body of the female does not bend, but rather remains tall and lengthened because the corset restricts bending from the waist. She can open her arms/palms like the man or bring her hand(s) to her bosom to show respect during the bow. Her eyes remain lowered for the duration of the bow.

Each actor should make subtle individual choices to make these manners and etiquette fit the character. But to bring the spirit and feel of the proper period to the production, the actors need to live within the rules, manners, and etiquette of Elizabeth's time. In many ways, the costume helps the actor accomplish this. The heavy, constrictive costumes of the Elizabethan era can be a useful, constant physical reminder of a different way of moving and behaving. For an actor with this mindset, moving believably in costume is not an encumbrance to be overcome, but rather a way to develop fully the character you are becoming.

15 | *Pulling Punches*

There are battles, both large and small, throughout Shakespeare. He wrote for an audience that expected and demanded exciting entertainment, and physical conflict on the stage answered that need. He wrote about violence for a society that frequently was violent. As modern television offers car chases, Shakespeare offered swordplay. The tragedies are full of bloody combat, and many—like Hamlet—end with the stage strewn with bodies. Titus Andronicus, Shakespeare's first theatrical success and the work that made his name, is full of bloody revenge, rape, dismemberment, cannibalism; the histories aren't far behind. A Shakespearean director must understand how to choreograph violence and, in addition to speaking the lines and being able to act, the Shakespearean actor must know how to fight.

An Introduction to the Basics of Safe Stage Combat

BRUCE LECURE

How do you advance the action with a realistic stage violence that the audience will believe but which will keep the actors safe from injury? If you choose to cut the violence, the scene does not climax properly. If you allow or encourage your actors to "wing it," you may have injuries, and perhaps a lawsuit, on your hands.

Because of the ultra-realistic violence we're accustomed to seeing in the movies, anything less than realistic on stage is not acceptable. If you use poor fighting techniques, your scene will look something like television wrestling and the whole illusion you've created for your audience will be lost. But if a fight during the climax of a play looks real and is executed safely, the audience's belief in the world of the play grows enormously.

If executed properly, the following techniques will help you create effective but safe illusions of violence on the stage.

The safest approach, of course, is to hire a certified fight director, take a workshop given by The Society of American Fight Directors, or take personal lessons from an expert in stage combat. However you learn the right moves, always remember that the most important principle of stage combat is safety.

The Fundamentals

There are two basic moves in stage combat: noncontact and contact. In noncontact moves, the illusion of violence is created by the way the move is staged, or what you allow the audience to see. Contact moves make actual contact to large muscle masses of the body, with a maximum contact of twenty-five percent of the total force of the move. Each and every contact and noncontact move needs to be executed flawlessly so it looks real yet is executed safely. There are several safety factors built into every combat move that should not be noticed by the audience but should protect the actors.

Actors always should make eye contact first. Only a brief exchange of glances is necessary before each combat move—but it *is* necessary. The eye contact keeps actors in sync with each other during a fight. Eye contact also keeps them safe when a problem arises. If an actor accidentally gets hurt prior to the fight or forgets a line in the middle of it, the other actor will see the terror on his partner's face and adjust accordingly, instead of continuing the fight as rehearsed.

This Hit Is a Miss

With noncontact moves, actors must maintain proper fighting distance. This means that a noncontact punch to the face, for example, actually "lands" no more than four to six inches from the face. The audience thinks it sees the punch hit the face, but it is an illusion, created by the way the punch is staged.

Beginning combatants need to practice measuring this distance. Actors should stand facing each other, with one actor extending a straight arm toward his or her partner with the hand closed into a fist. The other actor measures the four- to six-inch distance by placing an open hand to his or her face, with the thumb touching the nose, and extending the hand out to the full extent of the little finger. The combatant with the extended fist should adjust until the fist barely touches the edge of the open hand. After several hours of measuring the distance in this manner, actors will become accustomed to the spatial relationship between their bodies and easily find the proper fighting distance without measuring. The "victim" must remember *not* to lean into the punch.

Avoid Tension Headaches

Actors also must "act the tension." After they've learned the fighting techniques, most inexperienced combatants tend to "fight" with a great deal of tension in the body. This can be dangerous. If actors get too caught up in a fight scene, this tension will take over and they'll feel so much adrenaline that they lose their fighting technique and could injure another actor or themselves.

Actors must *act* the tension of the fight and keep their minds and bodies free. They need to keep concentrating on the fight's technical aspects. There always must be a balance between the acting and the technique; one must not rule the other. Physical acting exercises can be useful in learning to act the tension of a violent act.

Control Is Key

In fighting moves that require physical contact between combatants—such as a choke, hairpull, or shove—the "victim" must always initiate the movement and control the follow-through. This is exactly the opposite of what we are accustomed to in real life and so must be reinforced in rehearsal.

If Actor A must choke and push Actor B across stage during the choke, the victim—Actor B—controls the backward movement across the stage. Actor A must make it look as if he is pushing the other person while in actuality, the victim is pulling. This allows for more control and, therefore, safety.

In contact punches or kicks, "energy pullback" is essential. First, contact punches or kicks are only thrown to large muscle masses (for example, abdominals, quadriceps, trapezius muscle of the back), never to more sensitive areas such as the face or ribs. Second, with contact punches or kicks, we use what's called the "25/75 percent ratio." That is, twenty-five percent of the full energy of the blow actually makes contact with the body; the remaining seventy-five percent of the actual energy of the punch or kick is dissipated as the receiver pulls back as soon as the blow hits the target area. This is critical and must happen as quickly as possible.

To be safe, you must understand the four parts of any stage combat move: windup, follow-through, "knap" (the audible sound of the
hand or foot hitting the body of the victim, artificially made in noncontact moves and naturally made in contact moves), and reaction
(physical and vocal).

The windup and reaction are the most critical of these four parts
to sell to an audience. The windup needs to be large and committed
in order to draw the focus of the audience to the impending violent
act. In this way, the windup directs the focus of the audience to what
you want them to see. The reaction needs to sell the pain of the
move to the audience, through both physical and vocal expressions
of pain.

In creating an effective illusion of a noncontact move, proper
staging is essential, so the audience is unable to tell that the punch is
not literally hitting the body. This is possible because the human eye
cannot judge depth accurately. The actors must be in places on the
stage so that the audience cannot see the fighting distance and the
knap in a noncontact move. If Actor A knifes Actor B and is responsible for the windup and the follow-through, and Actor B is responsible
for the knap and the reaction, Actor A must be upstage of Actor B
and on a slight angle relative to the audience. This way, the audience
cannot see that the blade of the attacker is actually passing four to
six inches upstage of the victim. In noncontact moves, pay special attention to the staging of the move so that you allow the audience to
see what you want them to see, as well as hide your technique from
their view.

Contact Versus Noncontact Moves

Noncontact moves work best in a proscenium-style stage, where the
audience is on one side and the action of the fight is on the other.
You also can use noncontact moves in a three-quarter–thrust stage if
the move occurs as far upstage as possible, so that audience members in the side sections cannot see the fighting distance or the knap.
Do not attempt to use a noncontact move in an arena or theater-in-
the-round configuration—the move won't work from at least one angle and the illusion will not be created for the entire audience.
Contact moves, on the other hand, will work from any type of stage
configuration. On an arena stage, I would confine myself to using
only contact moves.

The key to learning any stage combat move is patience and repetition. Practice each move slowly—actors should pretend they are

underwater. Practice it over and over again. Actors will be tempted to go all out and perform the move before they are ready, but they should resist the temptation to practice the move at full speed as soon as they learn it. Slow repetition gives the body needed time to learn the technique properly. This will help avoid accidents later on.

While practicing, keep concentration and focus levels high. Allow plenty of time to learn each move. When focus starts to fade, take a break.

Also beware of having too much fun in the learning. I have seen many actors have so much fun learning these techniques that they lose their concentration and come dangerously close to getting injured. Stay focused on the safety.

Knowing these basic principles of stage combat will help make your next stage fight realistic and make your audience gasp.

Leave Nothing to Chance | 16

Stage Fights Must Be Choreographed and Rehearsed to Be Realistic and Safe

EILEEN P. DUGGAN

"*T*here's always a way to give the illusion of violence instead of really doing it," says Michael Monsey, a St. Louis actor who choreographs fight scenes for schools, community-theater groups, and professional companies. "There's always a safe way to do it and yet make it look real."

According to Monsey, who draws on nearly twenty years of experience, the key to safe stage violence is choreography. Nothing should be left to chance. "It's not improvised," Monsey says. "It may look like it's spontaneous, but it's all choreographed specifically."

Look for Motivation

A director planning a fight scene—a slap, for example—must first find out the motivation, says Monsey, who was one of just twenty-two Americans at a recent international stage-combat workshop in London sponsored by The Society of American Fight Directors and its British and Canadian equivalents.

Ask why one character is slapping the other: why is there a conflict? Next, analyze what kind of stage will be used. Is it in-the-round, a proscenium, or a thrust? How the audience views the actors will determine to a great degree the type of staging you'll need to provide. Other factors to be considered are the stage surface, the set and furniture, props, lighting, and music (if the scene is to be choreographed to music).

You'll need to experiment with different ways to do the slap. The sound of the slap, called a "knap" in theatrical jargon, can be made by the slapper by hitting his/her own hand, thigh, or other part of the body. Or the actor being slapped may make the sound. Sometimes a person offstage can make the knap by clapping hands or slapping two sticks together, but this must be coordinated precisely. Otherwise, "If the actors are on stage left and the person who is supposed to give the sound effect is all the way on stage right, that's comedy, not drama," Monsey says.

In some cases, such as theater in-the-round, a real slap is required. For a real slap, cup your hand, look your partner in the eyes, and slap the cheek just above the jawbone with your cupped fingers. Start gently, increasing the force until you get a loud enough sound. This will smart and sting, but will not hurt like a full-palm slap.

"You are hitting them hard, but it takes the two actors working together to know how far they can go and control it. That's one of the very important elements of stage combat, controlling what you're doing," Monsey says.

"While experimenting, the director should watch the action from all angles and distances, to make sure it looks and sounds right."

Monsey offers some other tips:

- *Allow enough time to rehearse the violence.* "If there's a lot of violence, schedule more rehearsals and your show will be that much better," Monsey says.

- *Don't take anything for granted*, even if it's only one slap in a show. "If a character gets so angry at their lover that they finally erupt in a slap, that's important," Monsey says. There needs to be a clear build to the violent moment so that it's believable to the audience.

- *Actors should continue working on their violent acts to the end of the run.* Run through the violence before each performance, starting slowly, then a little faster, gradually working up to performance speed. That way, when the actors go on stage, they'll be able to perform well and safely.

- For large-scale combat, when more than two actors are fighting, *choreograph the action in different sections of the stage one at a time*. While somebody is running a sword through another character, four people can be lying on the floor recovering. This keeps the viewers focused on one action at a time, making sure they don't miss anything.

■ *Make sure that all stage weapons are in working order*. If an actor uses a sword on stage, be certain that a standby sword is accessible during the performance in case a blade breaks.

■ *Don't go too fast*. "Real violence goes very fast; it's over in a matter of seconds and you can't even see it," Monsey says. "But on the stage, we slow things down to about half or three-fourths the speed of real violence so the audience can see it. They want to see that he's getting ready to hit him, they want to see the hit, they want to see where he's hit, and they want to see the reaction of the person who's hit."

■ *Put more energy into your acting instead of the punch*. The intent is more important than the action itself.

■ *Use eye contact to cue your fight partner*.

■ *Don't wear nonessential jewelry*, such as rings, bracelets, or necklaces, unless they are a very important part of your character's paraphernalia. Jewelry can cause injuries to you or another actor.

■ *Trust your choreographer and partner*; know their style and idiosyncrasies.

■ *Keep proper fighting distance*, whether it's unarmed battle or sword-fighting. "If the fighters are too far apart, they're just going to be swinging at air, but if they're too close, it's going to look very messy and someone might get hurt," Monsey says.

■ *Stay in control*. "One of the hardest parts of stage combat for the actor is that there's this heavy-duty conflict," Monsey says. "Your character is doing violence to this other person for a reason—you're jealous of them or you want to kill them—they're the other family, they're the Capulets, they're the Jets, they're the Sharks, and your adrenaline is going. As an actor, that's what's going on with you emotionally, but you always have to be in control so that you're working with your partner."

In other words, remember that violence on stage is an illusion. "It's acting. We're not really fighting, we're not really angry at someone else."

17 Learning from the Pros

*A*ctors and directors who wish to make stage violence a specialty would benefit from studying dance, gymnastics, sport-fencing, boxing, or any of the martial arts, fight director Michael Monsey says.

The Society of American Fight Directors gives workshops around the country, teaching the basic level of slaps, punches, kicks, and weapon work. The Society also holds an annual three-week summer workshop in Las Vegas. The Society offers certification at several levels, beginning with Actor Combatant, followed by Advanced Actor Combatant, then Certified Teacher.

There are fightmasters in the society who have devoted their lives to making stage combat better at all levels—professional, movies, television, stage, Broadway, outdoor theme parks, big shows in Las Vegas, Monsey says. "They're continually trying to find new moves and new techniques."

Pulling Hair *18*

*In addition to general counsel about stage combat, an actor do-
ing Shakespeare must be familiar with specific techniques for individual acts of violence that occur in some of the plays. In the
next two chapters, we look at some of those actions.*

*A Violent Action Begins
with a Flick of the Wrist*

BRUCE LECURE

How do you pull someone's hair on stage without
losing a single follicle? You use the stage combat
technique called "the hairpull." Here's how:

First, keep two safety factors in mind. Begin by
establishing eye contact with your partner while you are
standing at arm's length away. Second, never permit your fingers to move in front of your partner's face. One errant flick of
the wrist could mean fingers in your partner's eye(s).

After establishing eye contact, raise your open right hand
vertically toward the top of your partner's head (follow the
outside of the body to avoid the face). Your arm should
straighten as it lifts and your wrist should twist to the right as
far as possible by the time your open hand reaches the top of
your partner's head.

Do not, at this point, rest your hand on top of your partner's head or slide your fingers into the hair. The initial
"pulling" of the hair actually occurs an inch or two above the
scalp, since we are merely creating the *illusion* of pulling the
hair. As soon as your hand is an inch or so above your head,
you'll need to execute two quick twisting motions simultane-
ously. Your wrist, now cocked to the right, snaps to the left as

your hand closes into a fist; your arm, now straight, bends quickly at the elbow. This quick twisting action of your wrist and arm is essential to create the illusion that you have grabbed your partner's hair, when in reality you have quickly placed your fist on top of the victim's head.

The victim must next do two things at once. First, vocally and physically, sell the pain of the hairpull—after the assailant's twisting action. The vocal part must be a very high and sharp nonverbal screaming sound (perhaps in a falsetto). At the same time, the victim brings both hands up and grabs the attacker's arm around the wrist while applying pressure straight down on his or her own head. In this way, the attacker's hand is anchored on the victim's head and won't slide around during the ensuing struggle. Do not move the body until the hands are anchored.

Once the illusion has been created and the pain is acted, you can decide whether to move while the hair is being pulled. Any movement needs to be choreographed and controlled by the victim—which is the opposite of what happens in real life. Allowing the victim to control the movement gives both actors a strong sense of safety (and the victim always knows if the attacker's hand is firmly anchored). Nevertheless, the attacker must move slightly ahead of the victim and create the illusion that he is actually pulling the victim by the hair, thereby controlling the movement. It is very effective if the victim rises on his or her toes in an attempt to lessen the pain.

The release of the hairpull should be planned and carefully choreographed as well. The attacker opens the fist at the chosen release moment and "throws" the victim away. Your fist should open during the release so that you do not pull out any hairs that might have been lodged between your fingers during the struggle. Make sure the victim continues to register the pain, as well as how much hair was "lost," moment by moment immediately following the release.

The hairpull can be a very effective combat move to use during a violent moment on stage. Just be sure that any movement during the hairpull is choreographed and well rehearsed by both actors. Each needs to know where the other is moving at all times—and then act as if they didn't.

He Who Gets Slapped 19
The Safe Way to Give Someone the Back of Your Hand

BRUCE LECURE

The backhand slap to the face—that dismissive, degrading movement—can be a very effective and safe noncontact move to use in a staged fight. Here are tips on how to do it:

The slap begins after the two actors establish a moment of eye contact and proper fighting distance. While that distance for other moves generally is four to six inches in front of the face, for a backhand slap, the four to six inches is along the right side of the victim's head (for a right-handed slap). The combatants therefore will be closer during a backhand slap than with other noncontact moves, such as a "cross right."

The attacker extends his right arm so that his right hand is the proper distance from the victim's ear. The success of the move depends largely on the attacker's hand passing through this space next to the victim's head. Then follow the standard four parts of a combat move [see Chapter 15, "Pulling Punches"].

The Windup

The windup comes from the whole torso, not just the arm. This movement must be large and quick in order to grab the focus of the audience. Your right foot should be forward and your left foot back, with the weight equally distributed between both feet. Keep the center of gravity low and balanced by bending your knees. Begin by dropping your right shoulder and arm on a vertical plane. Be sure not to turn your head and eyes away from your partner during the windup.

Follow-Through

As the torso lifts, your hand moves vertically toward and arches over the right side of the victim's head. The hand passes four to six inches away from the side of the victim's head. For the backhand slap, it is all right to shift the weight onto your front foot as you follow through. This will assure that the back of your hand moves along the side of the victim's face. If the hand is not far enough along the side of the face, we will see light between the fingers and the victim's face, thus breaking the illusion.

The Knap

As soon as the back of the hand has passed along the side of the victim's face, the victim makes the sound of the hand "backslapping" the face by snapping the left hand into the palm of the right with a quick flick of the wrist. The sound is called the "knap." The movement must be contained in the wrist only and be kept close to the groin area. The knap should not be visible to the audience, so minimal arm movement is critical. Make it happen with wrist movement only. If you keep your hands supple and free of tension, the knap will produce a sharp slapping sound.

Allow your right hand to follow to the point of "contact" (the side of the face), while your left hand stays by the side of the body. As soon as the sharp knap sound is made, the victim immediately begins selling the reaction.

The Reaction

The victim snaps his head to the left at a forty-five–degree angle and his right hand follows to the point of "contact." The victim must show the pain of the slap on his entire face and body, as well as through a vocal reaction. This vocal reaction should follow right *after* the knap and not cover the knap sound. This sound should be a rather high but loud nonverbal grunting sound. Do not use words to sell the vocal reaction—they sound comic. Play around with this sound on your own to discover what works best; just be sure to make it loud and powerful. From this point on, the victim's pain shouldn't just disappear, but should dissipate, moment by moment.

Since the backhand slap is a noncontact punch, proper staging is very important so that the fighting distance and knap are hidden from the audience's view. This slap works best on a diagonal, with the victim somewhat downstage of the attacker. Be sure all sides of your audience cannot see the fighting distance or the knap.

Rehearse this move slowly many times and step by step; work up to speed gradually.

SELLING YOUR SHAKESPEARE

Everything seems to be ready. Your production of As You Like It has been set during the Roaring Twenties, in a New York full of speakeasies and flappers. You've cut a little bit here and there and the running time is just where you want it. Your sword fights are set and your actors are ready.

But is your audience?

In Elizabethan times, the city fathers of London felt that play-going was an immoral activity, and so prohibited theater managers from advertising their productions and thus luring customers. (They managed to overcome that prohibition with trumpet fan-fares and raised flags.)

Fortunately, today we don't have those restrictions. But we do have other problems. How do you sell a Shakespearean pro-duction to an audience that is used to more modern offerings? How do you sell a four hundred-year-old work—even though you may have set it in more modern times—to an audience that wants the latest thing? How do you sell a production that some may believe is difficult and hard to understand—and, yes, boring?

Of course, publicizing and atttracting an audience to your Shakespearean production is in many ways much the same as publicizing and attracting an audience to any play in your sea-son. You use many of the same techniques—word-of-mouth, posters, press releases, season tickets, promotions, and so on. (For more on these techniques, see two other books in the Stage Directions series, the Guide to Getting and Keeping Your Audi-ence and the Guide to Publicity.) But the Bard, as noted previ-ously, is a unique case. Here are some answers to the challenges he presents.

Cooperation, Not Competition, Was Their Key to Success

*T*here are few things we at Stage Directions find more satis-
fying than cooperative programs that link theater companies in an effort to share resources and encourage more
community participation. The "Seemore Shakespeare"
campaign, run by theaters in the Akron-Kent, Ohio, area is a classic
example.

It all began one fall when Neil Thackaberry, executive director of
the Weathervane Community Playhouse, and David Colwell, manag-
ing director of the Porthouse Theatre Company, were talking about
various potential cooperative promotional ideas. "We decided to explore some of these ideas further over lunch," Colwell recalls, "and
we invited several other arts administrators from other local theatrical institutions, including Stan Hywet Hall, the University of Akron,
and The Players Guild."

The Promotion

From that luncheon came the decision to hold an informal media reception at which the group would announce a cooperative "Seemore
Shakespeare" promotion. The joint program included the following:
(1) a direct-mail campaign to ten thousand households using joint
mailing lists; (2) special advertising in the playbills of the participating theaters; (3) a special ticket-discount offer; and (4) a bookmark
distributed to libraries, bookstores, and other places.

The bookmark idea particularly shows what can be done in a cooperative venture. "Lisa Alter, general manager of The Players Guild,
arranged the printing of the bookmarks at no cost by having them
printed on the wasted trim around another brochure she had in production at the time," Colwell explains. "Each participating theater
company distributed several thousand bookmarks to bookstores,
schools, and libraries in their respective neighborhoods."

Five Shakespeare productions were first considered, but by the
time of the media reception, the number had grown to six. The first
five were *Julius Caesar* (Weathervane Community Playhouse), *Romeo
and Juliet* (Players Guild of Canton), *Measure for Measure* (University

of Akron), *Henry IV, Part I* (Stan Hywet Hall), and *Much Ado About Nothing* (Porthouse Theatre Company). (Later, the planned production of *Henry IV* was changed to *The Taming of the Shrew*.)

After the media reception, invitations were mailed, and a reporter in Alliance, Ohio, called to see whether Mt. Union College, located there, had been approached about the promotion. "When the reporter learned we weren't aware of the college's planned production of *Twelfth Night*," Colwell says, "he called Doug Hendel, director of the production, who in turn contacted us the morning of the media reception. We invited him to join the venture, and so that day there were six theaters represented at the reception. We highlighted the addition to the media as a concrete demonstration of the effectiveness and power of cooperative ventures of this type."

Winning Media Support

At the media reception, details of the special discount offer were announced: $2 off each ticket to one Shakespeare production when a ticket stub from any other participating Shakespeare production was presented at the box office. "We also announced our collective statement of purpose," Colwell says: "'We hope to raise the visibility of our institutions and to promote the enjoyment of Shakespeare in performance, and build a foundation for future cooperative ventures that will benefit the cultural life of our communities.'"

A one-page article in the Akron *Beacon Journal* with two photographs from the media conference reported on the reception and the Seemore Shakespeare venture. A news release, "Cooperation, Not Competition, Is the Key to the Future of the Arts," was distributed to the media members who attended the reception and was mailed to those who did not.

"Our Seemore Shakespeare promotion received further media coverage as well, particularly in the *Beacon Journal*," Colwell reports. "We were featured in the paper's weekly entertainment section. The front page used a color photograph from Weathervane's *Julius Caesar* with the caption, 'It's Hard to Beat the Bard: Local Stages Prove Shakespeare's Staying Power.' Inside there was a two-page article that included three photographs. Furthermore, on the front page of the main section was a banner with a small color photograph, with the heading, 'Area Big on Bard: Three Community Theaters Show Shakespeare's Plays. At Least Three More to Come.'"

In addition, Lisa Alter, of The Players Guild, arranged for an interview between local public radio station WKSU-FM and her artistic director, Rick Lombardo, who also directed *Romeo and Juliet*. "This interview was a direct result of the Seemore Shakespeare news release," Colwell says. "Ultimately, WKSU put together a three-minute news piece about *Romeo and Juliet*, as well as the Seemore Shakespeare promotion. It aired three times while that production was in performance. The Players Guild also got several R&J sound bites on WKSU during the run. Lisa is certain that the opportunity would not have materialized without the promotion. Their production of *Romeo and Juliet* was a blockbuster hit for them, something they had not originally anticipated."

Pleasing Results

Originally planned for one season, the promotion was "informally prolonged into the next season for three of the participants," Colwell says. "Weathervane, Players Guild, and Theatre Kent extended the Seemore Shakespeare offer by honoring the $2-off discount when patrons brought their stubs from one of the two other participating productions to the box office. In addition, each theater ran the revised Seemore Shakespeare ad in their playbills. By this means, three more productions were added, extending the Seemore Shakespeare promotion an additional seven months." The added productions were *A Midsummer Night's Dream* (Weathervane Community Playhouse), *Twelfth Night* (Players Guild of Canton), and *Romeo and Juliet* (Theatre Kent at Kent State University).

Among the seven organizations that took part in the promotion, about one hundred ticket stubs were redeemed at the various box offices. "Most of those represented a ticket purchase for at least two people," Colwell says, "so we feel relatively safe in projecting that at least two hundred people crossed over and tried out a second Shakespeare production at a different theater."

The only difficulty surfaced at the Stan Hywet Hall company, which has no walk-up ticket window for purchasing tickets in advance, Colwell explains. "Their reservations are done by telephone, supplemented by walk-up sales prior to curtain. For phone orders, ticket verification was not possible. Also, many patrons would reserve tickets, but would not mention the ticket-stub discount until they showed up at the theater on performance day, ticket stub in hand, to pick up and pay for their tickets. This caused some accounting problems."

In general, however, the participating organizations are pleased with the result of the joint promotion. "We all agree that collectively we generated much more press coverage for our individual shows, because of the Seemore Shakespeare promotion angle, than we would have otherwise," Colwell says.

The unanticipated success of *Romeo and Juliet* prompted The Players Guild to include *Twelfth Night* in their subsequent season, he reports. Both Weathervane productions, *Julius Caesar* and *A Midsummer Night's Dream*, enjoyed exceptionally good box office. The University of Akron's *Measure for Measure* played to packed houses. *Romeo and Juliet* at Theatre Kent enjoyed an exceptional three-week run in its 190-seat Wright-Curtis Theatre. The production "grossed nearly sixteen percent more than its nearest box-office competitor in that theater during a five-year period," Colwell reports. "The production also outstripped other Theatre Kent Shakespearean presentations during that same time frame by 13 percent capacity. *Romeo and Juliet* played to 97 percent capacity; its nearest rival was that theater's production of *The Tempest* several years earlier, which played to 84 percent capacity."

Mulling over the results, Colwell emphasizes that "the administrators of each participating theater feel that the promotion's success can best be measured in terms of increased community and audience awareness of our individual theaters and programs; increased media attention; and, increased communication, cooperation, and camaraderie among the theaters and their administrators."

In other words, everyone came out a winner—the theater companies, their audiences, and the community at large.

WHEN SHAKESPEARE'S THE MAIN COURSE

*M*ost theaters may mount one Shakespearean play a season, or perhaps two at most. In fact, for many theaters, it may be several years between their Shakespeares. In those cases, the theaters must frequently switch gears and start almost from scratch—learning how to wrestle with the Bard, how to direct or cut or act or design specifically for Shakespeare. Rightly or wrongly, the theater that has been doing *I Hate Hamlet* has to make an adjustment when it does *Hamlet* itself.

But what about the theaters that major in Shakespeare? What about the theaters that have the Bard as a steady diet? Or what about the one-shot theater, focused only on an individual Shakespearean work? How do they approach the challenges of the plays? While their goals frequently are similar to the general theater company, their frames of reference may be different. Yes, they also want to entertain their audiences and help their actors and directors and designers grow and learn. But with a different framework, how do Shakespearean-focused theaters deal with all these questions—and others, that are specific to them? The next few chapters offer some answers—answers that offer valuable information to the general theater company as well.

20 | *Summer with the Bard*

Ashland's Oregon Shakespeare Festival Sets the Standard

NANCIANNE PFISTER

"*A*ny plans for the summer?"
   "Yes, we're going to Ashland."
   "Lucky you! What will you see there?"
   That exchange, or something very close to it, takes place thousands of times a year, all over the country. Note that the second question is not, "What will you do there?" but "What will you *see* there?" And although the United States has nineteen other cities named Ashland, few ask, "Which Ashland?" It's assumed if you're going to Ashland, you're going to the Oregon Shakespeare Festival.

In fact, the city of Ashland has become so thoroughly identified with the nearly seventy-year-old festival that many people think the event is called the Ashland Shakespeare Festival.

The Oregon Shakespeare Festival traces its roots back to the Chautauqua Movement, which brought culture and entertainment to rural areas of the country in the late nineteenth century. Ashland's first Chautauqua building was erected in 1893, mostly by townspeople. In 1917, a round, dome-covered structure was erected in the place of the original Chautauqua building. The structure fell into disuse, however, when the

Chautauqua Movement died out in the early 1920s. The dome was torn down in 1933, but the cement walls remain standing today; covered with ivy, they surround the Elizabethan Theatre.

Angus L. Bowmer, an enthusiastic young teacher at what is now Southern Oregon University, located in Ashland, was struck by the resemblance between the Chautauqua walls and some sketches he had seen of Shakespeare's Globe Theatre. He proposed producing a "festival" of two plays within the walls, in conjunction with the City of Ashland's Fourth of July celebration. The city cautiously advanced Bowmer a sum "not to exceed $400" for the project.

The Oregon Shakespeare Festival was officially born on July 2, 1935 with a production of *Twelfth Night* followed by *The Merchant of Venice*. The festival covered its own expenses, even though it had to absorb the loss of the daytime boxing matches that the city—which feared that the plays would lose money—normally held on stage.

Sixty-five years later, OSF is the third largest employer in this city of eighteen thousand, says Diane Allen of the Ashland Chamber of Commerce; only Southern Oregon University and the public school system have more employees. In addition to the 350 permanent workers, OSF expenditures in the city exceed $12 million.

The city centers on the Bard of Avon, Allen tells us, "and that makes tourism our largest industry. Many who come discover all the other activities, like whitewater rafting, available in the area. OSF brings more than $90 million to the state. In the city itself, visitors spend $118 million, not counting the travel expenses that brought them here or their theater tickets. Each person sees more than one play, for a total attendance of 364,602." That's a hefty financial reward for a fete based on some plays written four centuries ago.

"Shakespeare is our standard and our inspiration," says Timothy Bond, an OSF associate director. "Therefore, great themes and great ideas are the net we put our fish into. Shakespeare was one of the great imaginators. His stories are open to anybody peopling his plays. His histories are the history of human conditions."

The OSF annual budget is $13.7 million, but Bond will quickly tell you Shakespeare is not about money. The plays are in the public domain and can be done by any theater company, regardless of its financial status. The only wealth you need is the talent to produce them. Bond offers some directing advice to those tackling Shakespeare.

"You have to tell the story, to stay truthful to the text, to trust it. These plays celebrate language. You have to take time to explore that language. Why did Shakespeare use this word in that way? You have to be open to diversity; it's the only lens through which we can look."

This emphasis on the richness of diversity, a relatively recent trend in education and the arts, has deep roots in OSF, as it echoes the thought of founder Angus Bowmer, a teacher and director. More than fifty years ago, he wrote that OSF "should be a theater that presents its audience with a wide variety of theatrical experiences, including those provided by the world's great playwrights of all ages. It should not be a platform for the exploitation of any single political, social, aesthetic, or religious thesis."

In the beginning, OSF offered only two shows. Now that the company mounts eleven productions, how does it choose the plays that will add to the rich Shakespearean base? Bond explains the process. "We have finished the Shakespeare canon for the third time, but we don't do them in rotation. We do Shakespeare on all three stages and choose plays that have relevance and work into the season with each other."

The play-selection committee, the Boar's Head, includes actors, producers, designers, and marketing personnel. Along with quality scripts, the group looks for variety and diversity of voices and ideas, as well as a mix of classic and contemporary works. During a recent season, OSF offered Shakespearean classics such as *Othello*, *Much Ado About Nothing*, and *Henry IV, Part 2*, along with a new translation of Ibsen's *Rosmersholm*, August Wilson's *Seven Guitars*, and the jazz musical, *Chicago*.

While it might seem gilding the lily for OSF to offer more than first-quality performances, an adjunct program, Summer Pleasures, renews the rich Chautauqua tradition, providing lectures, entertainment, and the interactive Talks in the Park. Other summer enrichments include performances by a youth orchestra or a dance troupe, readings of unstaged plays, and backstage tours.

Those who call Ashland home enjoy the richness of OSF's educational opportunities. One aspect of the Study and Exploration program offers adult-education classes with credits given by Southern Oregon University. When government funding to local school arts programs was cut, OSF responded with the Ashland High School Partnership in which a company member leads a master class through all aspects of the school's spring play. Another part of the program sent OSF actors to 290 regional schools last year. Matinees with half-price tickets, special training for teachers, and a summer seminar for high school juniors are just a few ways the teaching legacy of Angus Bowmer is honored.

OSF began as an outdoor summer theater event, and now operates eight months of the year—this in the Pacific Northwest, where wet weather is not only forecast, it's assumed. What happens when it rains during a performance? A rich sense of humor may be necessary. According to Bond, "If there's lightning, that's dangerous and we have to close the show, but we have extraordinarily faithful and diligent audiences. They come with raincoats and plastic bags to cover themselves. The actors take off their outer garments and put on rain slickers while they continue the performance."

For Bond and for many others across the country, the Oregon Shakespeare Festival is an abundance of riches.

21 | Training for the "Neo-Shakespearean Age"

At Southern Utah University, Students Focus on the Total Theater Experience

NANCIANNE PFISTER

"*I*t may surprise you to think that training for musical comedy is parallel to training for Shakespearean plays," says G. MacClain (Mac) McIntyre, head of the department of theater at Southern Utah University.

"Surprise" doesn't begin to cover it, so we listen and learn. "For both forms," says McIntyre, "the structure is episodic and abstract. Both paint visual pictures. Musical comedy does it with song; Shakespeare does it with dialogue. Because we understand musical comedy, we understand the poetic genre."

So convinced is McIntyre of this connection, so popular are the plays of Shakespeare in our time, he thinks that if our civilization were buried for two hundred years, the artifacts available to those who unearthed us would lead them to label us "the Neo-Shakespearean Age."

Fanciful? Perhaps. Is there any practical application for students? Absolutely.

"Classical actors are wanted for television because they bring stature to the roles," says McIntyre, his fervor apparent in his voice. "Our students train for the stage, where they have to learn to project their voices to an audience of seven hundred. They also train for film, so they learn to bring that voice to the intimacy of the camera. We are hands-on, production-oriented; we expect every major to work on every production."

Cross-Training Required

The Theatre Arts and Dance Department prepares students with a general foundation in theater. Graduates are not only skilled at performance in film, television, and on stage; each also knows how to run a box office, devise a marketing operation, and sketch a costume.

All actors are required to take at least one dance class. All dancers must take technical classes "so they learn not only how to find their light, but also how that light is used to enhance their costume and their dance."

Every SUU theater major learns how to conceive and execute a set design. For some, this is the most difficult part of their training, according to McIntyre, himself a designer. "We have students who can't conceptualize space relationships. When we have them sketch the set, they begin to learn. [They need to know this] so that when they are working in a hall with nothing but tape on the floor, they can visualize the elevation." The goal is that students will know how to work on a set so that when a director tells them, "Move stage left and give me some business," the action will be appropriate to the surroundings.

McIntyre cited two overall purposes of the SUU undergraduate program. "We want to place our students in graduate schools in order to further their education before becoming professionals. We also want to place our graduates in secondary education in order to teach other students. We recommend that students go to work in the industry. Later, when they tire of the gypsy life and want to settle down, we're hoping they'll return to train the next generation."

When they do, they will have learned much from their own good teachers, especially those who take their work beyond the classroom. "We're real-world–oriented," says McIntyre. "One of our acting coaches takes a quarter off each year to work in television. Another does commercials. Many of our technical staff work in summer stock or the Utah Shakespeare Festival."

It is almost always to the benefit of students to have faculty who work outside the campus. Aside from being familiar with up-to-date technology, such teachers are great mentors with connections that will guide students to useful alliances. They can also be relied on for the occasionally needed, but sometimes unpopular, reality check.

The Shakespeare Connection

Six shows fill the academic season from October to May, along with a program of one-act plays directed by students. Presentations include classic, modern, and musical shows. But you'll find no Shakespeare mounted during the school year; there is no need. Whether you're a student, a teacher, or a fan, summer is for Shakespeare.

In 1948 McIntyre founded, with Fred C. Adams, the Utah Shakespeare Festival. Adams now serves as executive producer. Though an independent production, the festival has close ties to SUU, giving summer employment to students, faculty, and staff. The event has grown to include a series of classes and workshops as well as six plays, four of them Shakespeare's. These last are performed in the Adams Shakespearean Theatre, one of the few such performance spaces with all the hallmarks of an Elizabethan theater.

"We didn't rebuild the Globe," says McIntyre. "A true Elizabethan theater has three things: open air, a thrust stage, and gallery seating. So authentic is the Adams that the BBC came here to film a project, inviting an audience to the filming. These actors teethed on Shakespeare, but were used to working on a sound stage. They needed us to remind them of the magic of live stage presentations."

As finance director for the festival, McIntyre knows that the event contributes more than cultural wealth to the Cedar City area, about 260 miles south of Salt Lake City. "The Utah Shakespeare Festival generates $1.5 million a week in tourist dollars. The retail-sales tax base for the festival is larger than the Christmas holidays'."

Festival classes include falconry, actor-training, storytelling, and stage combat. There are forums and camps for junior actors and for senior citizens. There are appreciation classes for novices and special workshops for high school drama coaches.

"If you've studied a collaborative art, you've learned collaboration skills," says McIntyre. "Our graduates will take this industry into a whole new dimension. They may have to retool into entirely new circumstances, but the relationship between mankind and itself has not changed."

Whether with the Bard or on Broadway.

Kids Strut Their Hour upon the Stage

You say your company can't do Shakespeare? It's too difficult for you. You can't do Shakespeare because you don't really understand what it's all about. You believe that only classically trained, greatly experienced theaters, directors, and actors can do the Bard. However, some companies have proven that they are exceptions to these commonly held beliefs. Here's proof that the most important qualities you need to focus on Shakespeare are commitment and enthusiasm.

Are These Second Graders I See Before Me?

A performance of *Macbeth* by seven- and eight-year-olds? Some might roll their eyes on hearing of such an idea, but not the staff of the Utah Shakespeare Festival, who saw in this unusual event one answer to the often-heard question, "Where are the community-theater players and audiences of tomorrow to come from?"

It all began at a Shakespeare Theatre Association of America Conference in Stratford, Ontario. Here Festival staff first saw the first and second graders from Hamlet School (an auspicious portent) in Stratford perform their version of *Macbeth*. The performance began, and within ten minutes the conference crowd was captivated by these small, unlikely thespians. Within twenty minutes the crowd was converted.

How had this extraordinary event occurred? Lois Burdett, a Stratford public school teacher (recently awarded Canada's Meritorious Service Medal for her work with children and Shakespeare), has for twenty years used Shakespeare to teach math, history, language, botany, and other subjects to her youngsters. When Gary Armagnac, the Festival's education director, saw these young actors (complete with a seven-year-old violinist playing Renaissance dance music), he was certain that his state's educational system could benefit from Burdett's ideas. He had been studying the objectives of the new Utah State Core Curriculum, which requires a blending of theater and art into everyday subject matter.

Armagnac invited Burdett to come to Utah to teach master classes to teachers during the Festival's summer workshop series. Armagnac then took it a step further. "I thought, why not invite the whole class to perform their *Macbeth* on our Globe stage, the Adams Shakespearean Theatre? We believe that schoolchildren are our audience members of today and tomorrow. And truthfully, this acting troupe is impossible to resist."

On the Canadian end of the project, a plane was chartered for the trip, Stratford parents signed on, the economic development director for Ontario joined in, bake sales were held, money was donated from local businesses, and other major funding was raised. To prepare for their journey, the children studied the culture and history of Utah and even recorded their own original song, "Going to Utah," which played on Canadian radio.

On the Utah end of the project, Armagnac raised additional dollars for chartered buses to pick up the group at the airport and for trips to parks. He received donated park passes, box lunches, and hotel accommodations. He also engineered "Bard Buddy" relationships with the Festival's *Macbeth* cast.

The Hamlet School gave four performances of its *Macbeth* while at the Festival and appeared in Cedar City's Pioneer Day Parade. Said Festival founder Fred C. Adams, "These children are a wonderful touchstone for everyone. Their passion, imagination, and commitment remind us of what is really important in life."

And where participants of tomorrow get their start. As Richard Monette, artistic director of the Festival, points out, "It is awfully nice to remind oneself where the magic begins. The magic, as it has for thousands of young people, begins right here, in Grade Two."

SHAKESPEARE, AS YOU LIKE IT

*T*here are so many plays—thirty-eight, including two collaborations, and not including the lost play, *Cardenio*—that it is almost impossible to cover every aspect of producing one of the Bard's works. What follows, then, over the next few chapters are some varied looks at different parts of the Shakespearean puzzle.

23 | Teaching Shakespeare

A Powerhouse Teacher/Director Fulfills a Dream

IRIS DORBIAN

Michael Kahn, artistic director of Washington, DC's The Shakespeare Theatre and Juilliard's drama head, is a man driven by a mission. Dismayed at how seldom American actors perform Shakespeare, Kahn is taking matters into his own hands: In June 2000, he inaugurated an MFA program at his theater, where twenty carefully selected actors undertake a year long immersion in Shakespeare and nothing else. The training program, dubbed The Shakespeare Theatre Academy of Classical Acting, is affiliated with George Washington University. Kahn, a veteran director of highly acclaimed Shakespearean productions, both on Broadway and in the most prestigious regional theaters in the country, will helm the topnotch faculty consisting of company members from The Shakespeare Theatre and a host of guest artists.

For Kahn, this seminal graduate curriculum is the realization of a long-running dream. It also resolves, he says, a perennial dilemma for American actors wishing to tackle the Bard. "If you were an actor and you just wanted to study Shakespeare, you would have to go to England. I don't see why American actors have to go to England to study something they're going to come back here and do," says Kahn.

Kahn's idea for the ACA crystallized as a result of his work at Juilliard, where he has been teaching for more than thirty years. "Juilliard is a BFA program and it's four years. But students don't only study Shakespeare," adds Kahn, "though they come out doing it pretty well. I thought there needed to be an MFA program for people who wanted to spend a year, six days a week, working on Shakespeare—and connected to a theater that I think does it pretty damned well."

What fueled Kahn's desire to initiate ACA is something that has stuck in his craw for years: the shortsighted notion of theater critics who believe that only British actors, with their much vaunted training, can do justice to Shakespeare. Kahn refutes this by explaining that the best actors he's worked with in Shakespeare, including Stacy Keach, Avery Brooks, Kelly McGillis, and Hal Holbrook—whom he recently directed in *The Merchant of Venice*—have all been Americans.

"I think American actors are quite as capable of doing Shakespeare as anybody," insists Kahn. "It's just that they haven't had as much chance to do it. It's not as easy for Americans [unlike English actors] because they're not brought up with it. However, when the actor has the tools to do it—the American energy, physical and emotional life, and imagination—it is fabulous!"

The actors Kahn has trained include a virtual pantheon of talent in American theater and film: William Hurt, Harvey Keitel, Val Kilmer, Kevin Kline, Patti LuPone, Christopher Reeve, and Robin Williams. His artistic leadership credentials are equally distinguished. In addition to the Shakespeare Theatre, Kahn has served as an artistic director at a number of critically lauded theaters, starting with the now defunct American Shakespeare Theater in Stratford, Connecticut (a post he held while also working as producing director of New Jersey's McCarter Theater), and the Acting Company. He has been showered with numerous laurels for his exceptional body of work, and was the recipient of the first annual Shakespeare Globe Award.

Admission to ACA will be by audition, which consists of several classical pieces and one monologue from a modern play. Aspiring students also will have to compose an essay and furnish two professional recommendations to support their applications. The qualities that Kahn will be seeking when selecting students are the same qualities he always seeks when auditioning actors for any Shakespearean production: the ability to handle verse, a well-modulated voice, a flexible body, and a facility to make words—even those spoken in iambic pentameter—sound like they are directly issuing from the actors' own mouths and not from a text.

"I think that actors should realize that if they do Shakespeare, they should study and they should go to places where they will get training for their voice and understand the form in which these plays were written," says Kahn. "Because just saying, 'Okay, I want to do Shakespeare' and then mangling a production, wondering why it was so hard, will not only discourage an actor, but discourage audiences as well."

Making Shakespeare more accessible and less intimidating to students can only happen in the public schools, adds Kahn. "The kids should read Shakespeare aloud in class," he says. "They shouldn't worry about footnotes. They should be thinking about the stories and relationships, and not worry so much about the language."

Kahn would also like to see children attend more Shakespearean productions. He feels that the more young people are exposed to Shakespeare, the less likely they will grow up feeling alienated or overwhelmed by his plays. "I also think that some of those kids will also turn out to be actors. So it's important that Shakespeare itself should be somewhat demystified and made into what he was—which was a living, breathing playwright who wrote damned good stories and knew a lot and could be exciting, touching, and moving."

The positive reaction generated by a recent Juilliard production of *Macbeth* performed for two hundred disadvantaged students instills Kahn with hope. "Now those young people are going to start thinking that Shakespeare is not so bad," he reflects, "and they might actually start reading."

Books on Shakespeare Performance

24

17 Useful Resources for Actors and Directors

STEPHEN PEITHMAN

*T*here certainly is no shortage of books about Shakespeare or his plays. However, useful books on staging or acting in a Shakespearean production are not always easy to find. The following list includes titles reviewed favorably in *Stage Directions* magazine. All may be ordered through your local bookstore or favorite online book dealer.

John Gielgud lived and acted the life of Shakespeare longer than Shakespeare did. Until his recent death, he was indisputably the world's leading Shakespearean actor, tragedian and comedian. Ever since his headline-making first London performance as Hamlet in 1934, he had been acclaimed in role after Shakespearean role. Who better to explain what it is to so intimately inhabit the skin and brain and literary offspring of the world's greatest playwright? John Gielgud's *Acting Shakespeare* is a vastly informative and entertaining account of acting in Shakespeare's plays. [ISBN 1-55783-374-5, Applause Theatre Books]

In *Acting With Shakespeare: The Comedies*, actress Janet Suzman has crafted a superbly concise and clearly written account of how to develop fully realized characters in Shakespeare. Using a direct, practical approach, she examines Shakespeare's text with extensive line-by-line analysis of *As You Like It, Much Ado About Nothing*, and *Twelfth Night*. In so doing, she provides a veritable blueprint for developing fully considered and realized characters for the plays. Her discussion of the differences between tragedy and comedy is particularly enlightening. [ISBN 1-55783-215-3, Applause Theatre Books]

Typically, actors asked to audition with a Shakespearean monologue pick the same ones. To help the actor set himself apart, *Alternative Shakespeare Auditions for Men* [ISBN 0-87830-075-9, Routledge] begins with a list of monologues that are used too frequently. Then editor Simon Dunmore presents fifty speeches for men from plays frequently ignored, such as *Titus Andronicus, Pericles*, and *Love's Labour's Lost*. He also includes good but overlooked speeches from the more popular plays. In *Alternative Shakespeare Auditions for Women* [ISBN 0-87830-076-7, Routledge], Dunmore does the same for female actors, with speeches from *Coriolanus, Pericles*, and *Love's Labour's Lost*, plus less familiar speeches from well-known plays. In both volumes, each speech is accompanied by a character description, brief explanation of the context, and notes on obscure words, phrases, and references.

Clamorous Voices: Shakespeare's Women Today is an excellent resource for actors and directors. Carol Rutter addresses interpreting Shakespeare on stage from a woman's point of view, reactions, and feelings. We turned to that most problematic of Shakespearean characters—Katherine the shrew—and were struck immediately by the insight offered by three actresses who have portrayed her. Similarly, the book offers new readings of Lady Macbeth, Isabella, Rosalind, Celia, Imogen, and Helena—at once "radical" yet without changing the essence of Shakespeare's intent. [ISBN 0-70434-145-X, Trafalgar Square]

Discovering Shakespeare, a series of workbooks for students and teachers, is by actors Fredi Olster and Rick Hamilton. In each case one gets an abridged version of a play plus a vernacular translation, stage directions, and helpful background information. For example, in *The Taming of the Shrew*, we find articles on Shakespeare's sources and the meaning of the play, as well as Elizabethan marriage customs and an extensive analysis of each of the main characters. Olster and Hamilton also give a description of each scene, plus tips for rehearsals, character development, Shakespearean acting, costumes, sets, and props. All this is presented succinctly and clearly, with obvious passion and commitment. Published by Smith & Kraus, titles include *Discovering Shakespeare: Romeo and Juliet* [ISBN 1-57525-044-6]; *Discovering Shakespeare: A Midsummer Night's Dream* [ISBN 1-57525-042-X]; and *Discovering Shakespeare: The Taming of the Shrew* [ISBN 1-57525-046-2].

Free Shakespeare, by John Russell Brown, is meant to liberate the works of Shakespeare from directors and academics who seek to impose their ideas upon the plays. Brown strives to empower actors and readers to approach the plays armed with the many different interpretations inherent in them. Cited by many critics as a benchmark for the understanding of Shakespearean performance in the twentieth century, the newest edition also explores the technological and funding challenges facing Shakespearean productions in the twenty-first century. [ISBN: 1-55783-283-8, Applause Theatre Books]

Freeing Shakespeare's Voice: The Actor's Guide to Talking the Text, by Kristin Linklater, discusses the importance of language—sound, rhythm, and content—in Shakespeare's plays. She explains vowels and consonants, words and images, figures of speech, verse and prose speech, iambic pentameter, rhyme, line endings, and verse and prose alternation. Most interesting, perhaps, she helps the modern actor see his or her place in Shakespeare's world, as well as Shakespeare's voice in today's world. [ISBN 1-55936-031-3, Theatre Communications Group]

Finding good material for scene study, monologue work, and auditions is a constant challenge for actors interested in Shakespearean roles. *A Guide to Scenes & Monologues from Shakespeare and His Contemporaries*, by Kurt Daw and Julia Matthews, makes that job a whole lot easier. This is a complete guide to more than six hundred scenes and monologues from Shakespeare and his contemporaries—the most extensive offering available in one place. The authors have grouped the plays into traditional categories: comedies, tragedies, histories, and romances. From there, categories are broken down into further groupings (in the case of tragedies, for example: revenge tragedies, major tragedies, tragedies of classical times, and Jacobean tragedies). Short overviews are provided for each grouping, with individual introductions for each play. At the end of each section is a list of suggested excerpts suitable for use in auditions, monologue work, and scene study. Both beginning and seasoned actors will find this a valuable resource for making intelligent decisions about the roles they choose. [ISBN 0-325-00015-8, Heinemann]

Players of Shakespeare 3, edited by Russell Jackson and Robert Small-wood, offers intriguing essays on Shakespearean performance by actors with the Royal Shakespeare Company. Their insights are as various as the actors themselves, with a fascinating spectrum of approaches to Shakespearean roles, making this a highly useful resource. [ISBN 0-52147-734-4, Cambridge University Press]

Renaissance Drama in Action, by Martin White, is an introduction to Elizabethan and Jacobean theater practice and performance. White covers playhouse design, staging and rehearsal practices, verse and language, and acting styles. He also relates the Renaissance theater to the ways in which plays are staged today. Looking at familiar plays such as *The Duchess of Malfi*, *The Changeling*, and *'Tis Pity She's a Whore*, as well as less well-known texts, White provides an excellent overview as well as specifics. [ISBN 0-415-06739-1, Routledge]

Playing Bit Parts in Shakespeare, by M. M. Mahood, is a unique survey of the small supporting roles—such as foils, feeds, attendants, and messengers—that appear in Shakespeare's plays. Mahood explores the different functions of minimal characters and looks at how they can extend the audience's knowledge of the social setting of the play. [ISBN 0-41518-242-5, Routledge]

Scenes from Shakespeare: Fifteen Cuttings for the Classroom is a collection of fifteen short scenes from *Romeo and Juliet*, *The Merchant of Venice*, *Julius Caesar*, *Othello*, and *Hamlet*. Editors Michael Wilson and Theodore O. Zapel introduce each scene with a well-written plot synopsis and descriptions of the characters. As its title suggests, this is designed for classroom use, although it also would be helpful for workshops or group study. [ISBN 0-91626-090-9, Meriwether]

The Shakespeare Dictionary is a comprehensive guide to the Bard's plays, characters, and contemporaries. (In fact, its full title is *A Dictionary of Who, What, and Where in Shakespeare: A Comprehensive Guide to Shakespeare's Plays, Characters, and Contemporaries*.) Author Sandra Clark has done a great favor for actors, directors, and teachers. Not only is there an A-to-Z section of names and titles, but there also is a short biography of Shakespeare, a chapter on theater and play production in Shakespeare's time, another on his major poetry, and an annotated bibliography. [ISBN 0-84425-757-5, NTC Publishing Group]

In Shakespeare Sounded Soundly, author Delbert Spain provides a guide to the rhythm of the playwright's dramatic verse. Written from the actor's perspective throughout, the book includes a brief list of proper pronunciation of many words that differ between their Elizabethan and current usage. Where there is disagreement among various scholars, Spain duly notes it and gives what he believes to be the best solution for the actor. This is good work indeed. [ISBN 0-88496-274-1, Players Press]

In *Shakespeare's Plays in Performance*, John Russell Brown looks at the fuller meaning of Shakespearean text in its natural habitat—the stage. Brown, former associate director with London's National Theatre, has reworked his original 1966 edition to include recent productions at the Hartford Stage, Theatre for a New Audience, and the New York Shakespeare Festival. He also adds four new chapters, including the nature of speech in the plays and the theatrical element of Shakespeare criticism. Of special note are his discussions of gestures and stage business, and interplay with other characters. Directors will appreciate his discussions of focus, setting, grouping, movement, and tempo. [ISBN 1-55783-136-X, Applause Theatre Books]

Staging in Shakespeare's Theatres, by Andrew Gurr and Mariko Ichikawa, brings together evidence from different sources—documentary, archaeological, and the play texts themselves—to reconstruct the ways in which plays were staged in the theaters of Shakespeare's own time. In so doing, the authors show how the physical possibilities and limitations of these theaters affected both the writing and the performances. The book explains the conditions under which the early playwrights and players worked, their preparation of the plays for the stage, and their rehearsal practices. It looks at the quality of evidence supplied by the surviving play texts and the extent to which audiences of the time differed from modern audiences. It also gives vivid examples of how Elizabethan actors made use of gestures, costumes, props, and the theater's specific design features. Stage movement is analyzed through a careful study of how exits and entrances worked on such stages. The final chapter offers a thorough examination of *Hamlet* as a text for performance in its original staging at the Globe. [ISBN 0-19871-158-1, Oxford University Press]

Did You Know?

The "Did You Know?" department was a prominent feature of *Stage Directions* for the magazine's first decade. With short items about sundry theatrical subjects gleaned from companies across America, various readings, conversations, and other sources, "Did You Know?" offered an assortment of perspectives. Here are some hints, tricks, and pieces of advice on many different aspects of putting on a Shakespearean play, culled from more than ten years of "Did You Know?".

Shakespeare Reclothed

"I always like to do Shakespeare in modernish dress because I want to put people into clothes rather than costumes," director-actor Ian McKellan told the *San Francisco Chronicle*. "It's a shorthand storytelling device. You can tell by what somebody is wearing how much money they've got, whether they've got taste, whether they are in the military or a civil servant or an aristocrat. If you put everybody in pageant costume and floppy hats and tights and hands on hip, you don't know who the hell anybody is."

Follow the Leader

Director Jack Lynn believes Shakespeare used his leading character to tell his company how to act. Nobody can teach acting, he says. "There's no such thing as an acting teacher. There's an instructor, someone who guides. The talent has to be there and developed into a skill. If there were one single thing that *can* teach what acting is all about, it's dear old Shakespeare in Hamlet's advice to the players: 'Speak the speech, I pray you, as I pronounced it to you. . . . ' [Act II, ii]."

Stylish Selling

During its 35th-season celebration, the Utah Shakespeare Festival launched a series of clever promotional programs for its ticket sales. These are good ideas for any company producing works by the Bard.

Henry Night. If your name is Henry, Henrietta, or Hank, you get half off a ticket to *Henry IV, Part 1*. A picture ID is required to get the special price.

Twin Day. If you're a twin, your ticket for the matinee of *The Comedy of Errors* is half price. To purchase the ticket, you must present a photo of you and your twin, or you must bring your twin with you.

Celebrating Your 35th. Anyone celebrating a 35th birthday or wedding anniversary any time during the season may purchase a half-price ticket to *The Winter's Tale*. To purchase the ticket, you must bring a picture ID or a wedding certificate.

Mac Day. If your last name contains "Mac" (for instance, MacDonald or McMillan) or your first name is Mac, you get a half-off ticket to *Macbeth*. A picture ID is required.

Fancy Free

Arthur Oliver, resident costume designer at Massachusetts' Shakespeare and Company, has some useful advice for the costume designer at a small regional or community theater who'd like to design something elaborate or unusual but can't—due to a limited budget. Oliver advises to not "go out looking for fancy fabrics, such as silk or velvet. Just go out and use sheets or a tablecloth—yes, a tablecloth. As long as you know how to drape it, go simple, but make it look extraordinary. That is where your challenge will be. You don't need a lot of money to make great costumes. I know that."

Trippingly on the Tongue

Royal Shakespeare Company director Adrian Noble has devoted much attention at the company to teaching his actors the special talent of speaking Shakespeare's verse properly. It's an art, he agrees, that some people believe impossible for an American actor to master.

But it shouldn't be, he told a newspaper reporter. "The kind of whole, wonderful energies inside the American accent and dialects should be good for Shakespeare. But you need to harness the rhythmical energy of Shakespeare to that accent, and for some reason that's difficult—maybe because American actors try to play naturalistic, the whole modern Stanislavsky tradition, and Shakespeare was writing for a very different kind of actor. He wouldn't have understood 'characterization,' having provided the information and the psychology of the character within the dialogue."

Hair Apparent

When costuming a Shakespearean play set in the Elizabethan era or any past era, don't forget the hair. Mike Beecham, of the Atlanta-based costume shop, Production Values, says hair can make or break the look of a production. "I've seen period shows where the silhouette is fine, where all the appointments are there, but where the hair is perfectly modern," Beecham says. "It absolutely ruins the look."

Free Willy

More than twenty thousand students, educators, and administrators were entertained and educated by "A Rough Form of Magic," the eighth season of Shakespeare-in-the-Schools presented by the Shakespeare Festival of Dallas. Presented at minimal or no cost, the tour used the Bard's text and an original and innovative script to introduce students to the theatrical arts and to the importance and relevance of Shakespeare's works. In addition to an introduction to *Macbeth* and *Twelfth Night*, the students were given workshops on stage combat and iambic pentameter.

Each student received a study guide as well. The guide, called

The Bard's Bulletin, was written specifically for students in Grades 7–12, and donated by the *Dallas Morning News*, which printed twenty-five thousand copies. Design for the publication was donated as well.

To Bi or Not to Bi?

A recent production of *Hamlet* at Contra Costa College in California, according to its press kit, promised that "Prince Hamlet will be played by a Japanese American actress as a man. Polonius will be played as an adulterous sexual woman. Horatio, Hamlet's best friend, will be played as a woman in the style of Eve Arden and Rosalind Russell."

The play also featured "shocking and disturbing directorial choices." We certainly hope so, considering the ho-hum casting.

Best for the Bard

Shakespearean director Jack Lynn believes there's no such thing as a Shakespearean actor. "Laurence Olivier was known as one," he says, "and John Gielgud was known as one. But you are a great actor if you can portray *any* of the periods from the Greek through to the modern day. You become limited if you are called a Shakespearean actor or a 'modern actor.' Rex Harrison was a marvelous actor, but not a great actor, in my opinion, because he never would do Shakespeare and claimed he didn't understand it.

"To be called a true or 'great' actor, somewhere along the line we know that they have done Shakespeare. It gives grounding to their other work; it provides a technique that makes doing modern plays so much easier. You learn how to breathe properly, how to phrase. The problem with the Method actors is that they can't do period stuff. I agree with Stella Adler when she said that it would take a hundred years to overcome what Lee Strasburg did to American acting."

Foot Faults

Shoes—which can be elegant or shabby, low-heeled or high-heeled, simple or elaborate—can be a useful indication of a wearer's stage character. When choosing shoes for an actor in a Shakespearean play, keep in mind how footwear might help the actor portray the character. Consider also that few articles are more closely identified with a period than the footwear of a particular time, and substitutions can look anachronistic. When you can't provide authentic-looking footwear, it may be best to use something nondescript that won't call attention to itself. For example, a black shoe of the wrong style will be less intrusive than if it were in white.

Make Theater Happen

Rosemarie Tichler, artistic producer of The Joseph Papp Public Theater/New York Shakespeare Festival, has this advice for others wanting to get into producing Shakespeare: Get working experience, which she calls "making theater happen." Students should see a lot of the Bard's plays, not just read and study drama. They need to learn what things work in the theater and what things don't work. She advises students to envision new interpretations of the classics.

Ready, Set, Emote

The Market House Theatre in Paducah, Kentucky, sponsors an annual Shakespeare Competition each May. Competitors perform a selection from any of the Bard's plays; solo performances must be under three minutes, duets under four. The winner's name is placed on a plaque in the theater lobby. MHT does not charge an entry fee, but such an event could be used as a fundraiser as well.

Uptight

Do your male performers in your next Shakespearean show balk at the idea of wearing tights? One high school instructor tells her male students that tights are just cycling shorts with feet, or the same garment football players wear under their uniforms to keep warm.

In Style

The great Shakespearean actor John Gielgud once defined "style" in acting as "knowing what kind of play you're in." The Bard's works demand a different style generally from the actor than do other plays. This is because the content of the plays differs widely, partly because Shakespeare is writing in a different context—time, place, social situation—and partly because Shakespeare has a different idea of the manner in which he expects the actors to relate to the audience.

The result, Shakespearean director Tyrone Guthrie once pointed out, is that an actor cannot successfully impersonate the different characters without quite drastic variations in both the imaginative and technical approaches.

Costumers Beware

Thinking of setting one of the Bard's works in the Elizabethan Era? Be careful when using old books as sources for costume designs, advises Stephen Rausch of Schenz Theatrical Supply. "Most books show haute couture of the day," he points out, "not what the average person was wearing. You need to do your research into the cultural life of the time—art, music, architecture, literature, social behavior, class distinctions, social conventions, fads, use of color," he adds.

Pomp and Pageantry

The Acme Theatre Company, of Davis, California, believes that pageantry is essential to producing Shakespeare—particularly if you want to attract audiences unfamiliar with the Bard's works.

The company, which consists of high school-aged performers, has mounted an *As You Like It* set in the 1920s, *The Comedy of Errors* set in the hippie-style 1960s, and *Twelfth Night* in a contemporary Caribbean setting. The cast of Acme's *A Midsummer Night's Dream* took lessons in primitive African street dancing to infuse the production with the cadences of a multicultural happening.

The extensive pageantry, says company director David Burmester, is a way to introduce the genre to those who might otherwise choose not to attend, especially younger siblings of the performers.

The Point of It All

Never forget that your motivation for producing a Shakespearean play is to entertain your audience—not to lecture them on important issues or impress them with your seriousness. Shakespearean theater, says director Jack Lynn, "must first entertain, then enlighten. These people who go around and say we've got to educate our audiences; I'm sorry, you've got to entertain them, and by entertaining them you'll educate them. Let's get it the right way around."

Final Thoughts

Critic and historian Gary Taylor puts it this way concerning the importance of the plays of William Shakespeare: "His works have become our secular Bible."

Even those who have never seen a Shakespearean play—or would even contemplate going—are familiar with the plots and know the famous lines. They know about *Romeo and Juliet* or *Macbeth*. They know—or think they know—what attending a Shakespearean performance would entail. It is a challenge, then, to mount a production that shows our audiences and potential audiences that it is, after all, much ado about something.

Contributors

DIANE CREWS is Executive/Artistic Director of DreamWrights Youth & Family Theatre, in York, Pennsylvania.

IRIS DORBIAN is Editor of *Stage Directions*.

EILEEN P. DUGGAN is the editor of a community newspaper in St. Louis, a freelance music critic, and a dresser and seamstress for several amateur and professional theater groups.

IVAN W. FULLER is a member of the faculty of Augustana College, in Sioux Falls, South Dakota. His doctoral dissertation was entitled *A Critical Case Study of Anachronistic Productions of Shakespearean Texts*.

BRUCE LECURE is Movement Specialist in the conservatory acting program at the University of Miami in Coral Gables, Florida.

JULIAN LOPEZ-MORILLAS is a professional actor and director with more than thirty years' experience in Shakespeare production. He lives in the San Francisco Bay area.

DALE LYLES is artistic director of the Newnan Community Theatre Company, in Newnan, Georgia. He recently celebrated his twentieth anniversary directing, and has staged more than one hundred productions.

NEIL OFFEN served as Editor of *Stage Directions* for five years. He is currently a freelance writer in Chapel Hill, North Carolina.

STEPHEN PEITHMAN is co-founder of *Stage Directions*, where he served as Editor-in-Chief for eleven years. He is currently Consulting Editor at the magazine.

NANCIANNE PFISTER served as Associate Editor of *Stage Directions* for eleven years. A teacher and freelance writer, she lives in Davis, California.

LINDSAY PRICE is artistic director of Theatrefolk, a company based in Toronto. In her spare time, she works as a playwright and teacher.

JAMES A. VAN LEISHOUT has served as Artistic Director of the Washington Shakespeare Festival in Olympia.

MORE BOOKS
from Heinemann's *Stage Directions* series
Stephen Peithman and Neil Offen, *Editors*

Stage Directions Guide to Working Back Stage

Learn how to create a truly collaborative and supportive back-stage effort. This book offers information on proper installation and maintenance of rope and rigging; safety guidelines for ladders, catwalks, and other high places; and more.

0-325-00244-4 / 176pp / 2000

Stage Directions Guide to Publicity

If your theater isn't on Broadway and doesn't have an expensive press agent (or ad budget), how does it get attention? That's where this book steps in, providing information on aspects of the publicity game.

0-325-00082-4 / 114pp / 1999

Stage Directions Guide to Directing

Every director—from the beginner to the most experienced—will find in this book invaluable information to make their direction more effective. Topics include things to look for in an audition, selecting the right play, criticizing effectively, and more.

0-325-00112-X / 168pp / 1999

Stage Directions Guide to Getting and Keeping Your Audience

How does a theater attract and maintain the audience it needs? You'll find out how in this book, discovering practical suggestions on advertising to motivate ticket-buyers, creating attention-getting mailings, and more.

0-325-00113-8 / 148pp / 1999

Stage Directions Guide to Auditions

Readers will discover expert advice on a range of audition topics, including choosing the right monologue, preparing your voice for auditions, steps to getting cast, sealing the deal at callbacks, and more.

0-325-00083-2 / 144pp / 1998

For more information about these books,
visit us online at **www.heinemanndrama.com**, call **800-793-2154**, fax **800-847-0938**,
or write: Heinemann, Promotions Dept., 361 Hanover St., Portsmouth, NH 03801.